Buffalo Board of Trade

The City of Buffalo and its Surroundings

Its Business Facilities and its Advantage as a Place of Residence and

Summer Resort

Buffalo Board of Trade

The City of Buffalo and its Surroundings
Its Business Facilities and its Advantage as a Place of Residence and Summer Resort

ISBN/EAN: 9783337193331

Printed in Europe, USA, Canada, Australia, Japan

Cover: Foto ©Andreas Hilbeck / pixelio.de

More available books at **www.hansebooks.com**

THE

CITY OF BUFFALO

AND

ITS SURROUNDINGS.

ITS BUSINESS FACILITIES AND ITS ADVANTAGES AS A PLACE OF RESI-
DENCE AND SUMMER RESORT—ITS RAILROADS, ELEVATORS AND
MANUFACTORIES—ITS SCHOOLS, CHURCHES, PARKS,
STREETS AND HOTELS—ITS LAKE, CANAL AND
RAILROAD COMMERCE, AND ITS
LIVE STOCK TRADE.

• • •   — -

BUFFALO:
PUBLISHED BY WILLIAM THURSTONE.
The Courier Company, Printers, 197 Main Street.

1880.

BUFFALO BOARD OF TRADE.

BUFFALO AND ITS SURROUNDINGS.

THE CITY OF BUFFALO.

BUFFALO for many years has been called the "Queen City of the Lakes," and well merits that proud appellation. It is a port of entry and the capital of Erie county, State of New York, at the eastern extremity of Lake Erie, at the head of Niagara River and at the mouth of Buffalo River, in lat. 42° 53′ N., long. 78° 55′ W., about 293 miles N. W. of New York city:— with a water front of two and a half miles on the lake and of the same extent on Niagara River.

Buffalo has one of the finest harbors on the lakes. It is formed by the Buffalo River, a small stream, which is navigable for about one mile from its mouth. The entrance is protected by a breakwater, which is 1,500 feet long, upon the south side of the river; and there is also another on the north side, by which a capacious harbor is made. In 1869, the United States Government began the construction of an outside harbor, by building a breakwater, designed to be 4,000 feet long, fronting the entrance of Buffalo River, at the distance of about half a mile from shore; nearly two-thirds of the breakwater is completed. In addition, there are a large number of slips, docks and basins for the accommodation of shipping and canal boats.

The advantages of Buffalo, in a commercial point of view, are obvious. Its location at the foot of Lake Erie, whose waters unite with the Hudson River and the seaboard by the Erie Canal, and the centering of many important railroads in its midst, are a sufficient assurance of a continuance of its present business prosperity and future growth.

The State census returns for 1875, places the population of the city at only 134,573 and of the county 199,570. The estimated population of the city on the first of January, 1880, was 155,000.

The earliest notice of the present site of Buffalo, may be found in the travels of Baron La Houtan. He ascended the Niagara River into Lake Erie, on the fifteenth of August, 1687, more than a hundred years prior to the first settlement of the city. He advised the French Government to build a fort here, and, in anticipation of its construction, named it "Fort Suppose" on the map accompanying his travels.

This fort was intended as a check against the neighboring Iroquois and Seneca Indians. In 1795, La Rochefoucault Lianconkt, a French nobleman, says that "at the port on Lake Erie (Buffalo) there was a small collection of four or five houses." On the map of the Holland Land Company's Purchase, drawn in 1800, the present site of Buffalo is designated as New Amsterdam. The village, however, was not laid out and the survey completed until 1804. The first lot sold contained half an acre and brought $135.00.

On April 2, 1813, the village was incorporated, and in the same year, on December 30th, was burned, with the exception of two houses, by a force of British troops and their Indian allies, who crossed from Canada at Black Rock.

In 1832, Buffalo became an incorporated city, and is now divided into thirteen wards, with two aldermen to each ward. The principal officers are a Mayor, Comptroller, Clerk, Attorney, Treasurer, Park and Street Commissioners, Engineer, Superintendent of Education, Assessors, Overseer of the Poor, Commissioner of Public Buildings, Board of Water Commissioners,

Commissioners of City and County Hall, and Police Justice. For Police purposes the city is divided into precincts. The Fire department is under the management of a Superintendent and assistants.

Previous to 1832 all the schools were known as district schools of the town of Buffalo. The first school-house was erected in 1806 by gratuitous labor and material contributed by the early settlers, and was located at the corner of Cayuga (now Pearl) and Swan streets. The number of public schools in existence, including the Central, January 1, 1880, was 44; number of teachers, 440; average number of pupils in attendance daily, about 15,000; and the amount paid for this department by the city for the year ending December 31, 1879, was $308,700.57, including salaries, $280,277.15. The State Normal School and Normal School of Practice is also located here. There are also about forty private academies, colleges and schools, including the Medical Department of the University of Buffalo, a college established for the study of medicine; the Homeopathic Medical Society and the College of Rational Medicine, the Buffalo Female Academy, the Buffalo Classical School, the Heathcote School, St. Joseph's and many other Roman Catholic schools, the Holy Angel's Academy, the Canisius and St. Joseph's colleges. These are all well patronized and are reported to be in good financial condition. It may be well to note that the Central Public School curriculum includes the languages.

The commercial advantages of Buffalo are well known, derived from its favorable relative position with the numerous points from which are drawn its receipts of flour, grain, coal, ore, oil, cattle, hogs, etc., and the ready means for the distribution of these articles by lake, canal and railroads; added to which facilities are the benefits of cheap fuel, an excellent and abundant water supply, rapid elevating and transfer of grain, quick handling of coal, extensive storage facilities and dockage with ample harbor accommodations. The healthy climate, (shown by its vital statistics,) handsome streets and driveways, magnificent park system, its public libraries, art gallery, museum, theatres, hospitals and benevolent institutions of all kinds, churches and fine public buildings, combine to render Buffalo a most desirable resort for the pleasure and health-seeker, and a home for the capitalist and the laboring classes. Its close proximity to Niagara Falls, added to the delightful and romantic lake and river scenery, contributes greatly to its attractions.

The Buffalo street railroads comprise two main lines, one 4¾ miles, and the other about 3½ miles in length. The branch lines aggregate nearly 9¼ miles of rail.

Buffalo ranks as the third city in the State, but in commercial importance she must be deemed second only to the metropolis. It is no wonder that her citizens are proud of her position and manifold advantages. With very few equals in the world as a grain port, its terminal facilities are very extensive and complete. Grain is received, transferred, stored and forwarded with greater dispatch than at any other port in this country. The river for about a mile from its mouth is lined with immense elevators and floaters, provided with all of the most improved appliances for handling cereals. The transfer of grain cargoes from vessels into storehouses and canal boats prior to 1843, was done by manual labor, being raised from the hold in tubs and bags. In that year Mr. Joseph Dart erected the first elevator ever built for storing and transferring grain, with a storage capacity of 55,000 bushels, and a transfer capacity of 15,000 bushels per day, near the mouth of Buffalo River. Now there are 20 elevators, 6 transfer elevators and 6 floaters, 32 in all, most of which are massive structures costing in the aggregate about $5,000,000. Their combined storage capacity reaches 6,265,000 bushels, while their daily transfer capacity is 2,500,000 bushels. That is to say, the elevators of Buffalo are capable of receiving from lake vessels and transferring to canal boats and cars nearly 3,000,000 of bushels of grain every twenty-four hours. Much has been said and written against these Buffalo elevators, but the fact that they furnish such excellent facilities to carriers and shippers, insuring quick dispatch and freedom from costly delays, is an advantage that can be scarcely overestimated. These elevators are owned by private individuals, excepting that the New York Central and Hudson River Railroad corporation owns two of the largest, and the New York, Lake Erie and Western Railroad one. Several of these elevators have machinery attached, whereby 60,000 to 70,000 bushels of wet or damaged grain can be dried every twenty-four hours. The grain trade has steadily increased for years. Last season's receipts were the largest on record, aggregating by lake and rail 140,000,000 bushels. The facilities for forwarding this vast amount of grain are as extensive as the terminal facilities.

The capacity of the canal has never been fully tested, and the shipments of 1878, which, were the largest ever reported, and reached 59,000,000 bushels, were forwarded with as little effort as the 36,000,000 bushels shipped in 1875. This fact is accounted for by the deepening and improvement of the canal so as to permit of the passage of boats with increased speed. The canal and railway competition thus afforded always insures cheap rates. The Central and the Erie railroads give much attention to conveying grain, and each moves large quantities received by lake as well as its through shipments. Their tracks run directly into the elevators, so that there is no carting and no handling outside of the elevator. It is no uncommon thing to see a large lake vessel being unloaded and two canal boats and two trains of freight cars being loaded at the same time.

There are four large steamboat lines plying regularly between this port and the ports of Lakes Huron, Superior and Michigan. They are the Union, the Western Transportation, the Commercial and the Anchor lines. Their combined fleets number several first-class steamers, some of which are as large as the average ocean steamships, having a capacity ranging from 2,000 to 2,500 tons. With the completion of the Government improvements in the Detroit River, which are well advanced, the appearance of 3,000-ton vessels in Buffalo harbor will not be an unusual sight. In addition to the vessels of these lines, there is an almost innumerable fleet of steam barges, with consorts, and sailing vessels, many of which are noble ships. With a heavy down movement of flour, grain, iron and copper ore and lumber, and a large and steady up movement of coal, salt and merchandise, Buffalo bids fair to always occupy a front place among the great commercial cities of the continent.

Manufacturing interests are attracting as much attention at present as the other branches of business mentioned. The admirable location for manufacturing and the necessity for diversified industries have induced Buffalo capitalists to invest large amounts of money in furnaces, rolling mills and factories of various kinds. With the lakes stretching to the westward and the canal to the eastward, together with the New York Central, the New York, Lake Erie and Western, the Buffalo, New York and Philadelphia railways leading East and the Lake Shore, the Canada Southern, the Great Western, Grand Trunk and the Buffalo and Southwestern running West, facilities are furnished for shipping manufactured products to all parts of the country, at low rates of freight that are not surpassed by those of any other city in the country. Buffalo, also, occupies a position between the coal and iron fields of Pennsylvania and Ohio, and the iron mines of Lakes Superior and Champlain that is very advantageous. The various kinds of iron ore required to produce the best results and coal and coke are laid down here at minimum rates. Manufacturing has made rapid strides of late years. The stove works located here are the largest in the world. The iron and nail and the malleable iron works, the planing mills, the grape sugar works, the chemical works and fertilizer works are among the largest establishments of the kind in the country.

To these must be added the car wheel works, the marine and other engine works, iron bridge building, the manufactories of water-mains and gas-pipes, chains, mills and mill-furnishing goods, threshing machines and agricultural implements, stamped hardware goods, refrigerators and bird cages ; tanneries ; boot and shoe and furniture factories ; soap makers; pork packing houses ; edge-tool and hinge factories ; children's and other carriages ; organs and melodeons are made extensively, and other industries too numerous to mention ; shipbuilding is also carried on to a large extent.

The wholesale mercantile establishments embrace every kind and the business transacted is immense. The banking facilities are very good, with an aggregated capital of $2,700,000, and other resources equally large. The last official returns from the four savings' banks show the deposits therein to aggregate $18,241,569. The three local insurance companies are prosperous and with a high reputation.

The three principal daily newspapers are the *Courier, Commercial Advertiser,* and the *Express* ; the first named is Democratic, the second and third Republican. There are several German dailies, besides many religious and secular weekly journals.

The total indebtedness of the city on the first of January, 1880, was $7,416,195.96.

The malting interest is a very important one ; twenty-four malt-houses were in operation last year, turning out over 2,000,000 bushels of malt, and the brewers manufactured 500,000 bushels in addition—a total product of 2,500,000 bushels. The imports of barley from Canada during the past season were about 1,220,000 bushels.

In the latter part of the year 1880 two pipe lines will compete for the transportation of crude petroleum from the Bradford oil district, and it is expected that the refining industry of this city will attain large proportions.

The Board of Trade is an important institution. Its rooms are situated at Central Wharf, on the river front. This organization was formed in 1844 and incorporated in 1857. It is expected that in the near future a handsome and commodious edifice will be erected up-town for the meetings of the members.

The East Buffalo live stock trade is of great importance. The yards for the accommodation of all descriptions of stock cover fifty-two acres of ground, are all paved and provided with the requisite sheds to protect stock from the weather and chutes for loading and unloading stock. This business gives employment to a large number of men and boys. Notwithstanding the great competition of rival cities, Buffalo has held its own as a center in the trade. Its present magnitude and recent growth is shown on page 22.

The system of water supply and works is one of the best on this continent and thus far have cost $3,000,000. The water is brought through a tunnel extending into the middle of Niagara River, thus insuring absolute purity. The construction of this tunnel and its inlet pier was a work of great magnitude, requiring the best engineering skill. The Holly Water Works system is also in use, and further improvements, at a cost of $250,000, are contemplated.

Another tunnel under the Niagara River, for railroad purposes, is often talked of and its construction is only a question of time, since the great International Bridge is inadequate to the accommodation of all the railroad traffic between Buffalo and Canada. This bridge was opened November 3, 1873, and was built by a joint Canadian and American company, at a cost of $1,500,000. It is nearly three-quarters of a mile in length, and the construction of the central portion was attended with great difficulty, owing to the rapid current of the river.

Among the institutions in which special interest is taken are the Young Men's Association, with its large circulating library ; the Society of Natural Sciences, which possesses a fine museum, free to the public ; the Grosvenor Library, another free institution : the Historical Society, the archives of which are full of valuable material relating to the early history of the city and of Western New York ; the Fine Arts Academy, which owns many fine works of art, and the Decorative Art Society, which is doing excellent work.

The Buffalo Driving Park Association has one of the best and fastest tracks in the country. It is the track on which Dexter's and Goldsmith Maid's best records were made, and on which Rarus trotted in the unequaled time of 2.13¼—the fastest on record. Buffalo also boasts a first-class base ball club, a well-organized yacht club, rowing clubs, archery clubs, the polo club which defeated the Westchesters, with James Gordon Bennett, Esq., at their head, and other similar organizations.

The City and County Hall, built at a cost of $1,400,000 and dedicated in March, 1876, stands on a site bounded by Delaware, Franklin, Eagle and Church streets, and the surrounding grounds are laid out and terraced in an artistic and ornamental manner. The building is of granite, with a tower containing an electrical illuminated clock, and is adorned with four representative statues. It is three stories high, not including a finished basement, and furnishes quarters for all the city and county officers as well as the courts. The Common Council Chamber is very handsome and commodious. The new Jail, finished last year, stands at the junction of Delaware and Church streets, facing the City Hall. The two buildings are very similiar in external appearance, and are connected by an underground passage.

The State Insane Asylum is slowly progressing toward completion, and is an ornament to the locality where it is located. The Erie County Penitentiary and the Almshouse are model institutions of their kind; the latter has an insane asylum attached.

The several hospitals, the homes for invalids, women and children, the deaf and dumb and orphan asylums and kindred benevolent associations are well managed and have comfortable and roomy buildings.

The Charity Organization, the Guild of the Good Samaritan and the Crèche are admirable institutions, and were founded under the auspices of the Rev. Stephen Humphreys Gurteen.

There are many fine edifices in the city, among the most prominent are the Custom House, the German Insurance, Manufactures' and Traders' Bank and Young Men's Association Buildings; the Erie County, Western and Buffalo Savings Banks and Pierce's Palace Hotel.

The new depots of the New York Central and Erie railroads are commodious and ornamental. Several of the banks are located in very handsome edifices, and many merchants have imposing business blocks. The buildings of the *Courier*, *Commercial Advertiser* and *Express* newspapers indicate prosperity. The Academy of Music is old-fashioned exteriorly, but the interior is all that could be desired, both for the comfort of the audience as well as for scenic representations, and is ably managed. St. James Hall has been renovated and improved, with new scenery added, and meets all the requirements necessary for comfort. The Adelphi Theatre is a cosy place and successfully carried on.

Buffalo has long been celebrated for the elegance of its private residences, which can be found in nearly every part of the city, especially on Delaware, Main, Franklin, North, and other avenues on the west side. The grounds attached to these homes are kept with great care. The noble trees which line the walks of the main thoroughfares add greatly to the beauty of the city.

The churches and places of worship number over one hundred, divided according to denominations as follows : Catholic, 21; Episcopal, 12; Baptist, 11; Methodist, 15; Presbyterian, 12; Jewish, 3; Universalist and Unitarian, 3 each; Lutheran, German Evangelical and all others, 25. The most beautiful edifice in the city is St. Paul's Cathedral (Protestant Episcopal); it is a brown stone edifice of the Gothic style of architecture, and has a tall, graceful spire, containing a fine chime of bells. A stranger passing though Main street during the warm months will have his attention attracted to the church by the loud twittering of hundreds of swallows who make their nests in the mass of foliage which has grown over the chancel walls. St. Joseph's Roman Catholic Cathedral and the episcopal residence adjoining are imposing piles of light-colored stone. The cathedral is noted for its chimes. St. Louis and St. Mary's Roman Catholic Churches, St. John's, Ascension and Christ Episcopal Churches, Westminster Presbyterian and Delaware Avenue Methodist Episcopal Churches are all fine edifices and the interiors are beautiful in decoration and furniture.

The city of Buffalo has all the favorable conditions for health, longevity and mental and physical vigor that can be desired, unequaled by any city in the United States. The climate is salubrious, of a uniform temperature, without extremes of either heat and cold, the mercury scarcely ever rising above 84 degrees or falling below zero. The death-rate is as low as any city in the world, only 13.9 per 1,000. It has many special advantages as a summer resort, which of late years have been quite largely appreciated. Situated within twenty-two miles of Niagara Falls, the trip by rail on the several railroads is too short to be fatiguing, and the return trip in the evening is always pleasant, as the traveler gets the benefit of the fresh air from Niagara River during most of the distance. The drive to the Falls is very fashionable at times during the season, and when the grand idea of a boulevard connecting the city with the village of Niagara Falls is realized, it will be still more so. On Grand Island there are several private club houses and places of resort. Everybody in Buffalo goes "down the river" more or less during the season, and several wealthy citizens own private steam yachts. One of the most attractive drives is that which leads to the "Front"—now a part of the park system—a noble bluff above the bank of the Niagara, which commands an extensive view of the lake and river, and also of the harbor and portions of the city. The tall tower of Pierce's Palace Hotel is close by, and from that elevated point on a fine day the distant Chautauqua hills are visible in one direction, and the spray of Niagara Falls can be seen in another. Buffalo is about seventy miles distant by rail from Chautauqua Lake, while a trip of less than thirty miles will take the traveler to Lewiston, Niagara City, and the shores of Lake Ontario. These points are much visited during the season by excursionists. The distance by lake from Buffalo to Cleveland is 174 miles, to Toledo 264 miles, to Detroit 255 miles, to Bay City 463 miles, to Chicago 888 miles, to Duluth 991 miles, and to Milwaukee 823 miles.

An act authorizing the selection and location of certain grounds for public parks, and to provide for their maintenance and embellishment, was passed by the State Legislature in 1869, and lands were selected and appraised at $305,157.85. Messrs. Olmsted & Vaux, of New York, were engaged to prepare plans; Mr. Geo. R. Radford was selected as engineer and Mr. William McMillan was secured as superintendent. No time was lost in getting the great work under way, and to-day the city has a park on a scale sufficient to meet the demands of a large and rapidly-growing population and one that will compare favorably with any on the continent.

8

The commissioners have always been mindful of the public interests and have fully appreciated the responsibility of their position. There has been no lavish expenditure of money and good judgment has characterized their work. The total area of the lands used is 600 2-10 acres, embracing the Lake, Meadow, Parade, Front, Niagara square, Prospect hill, North street circle, Bidwell place, Chapin place, Soldiers' place, Agassiz place, the Bank, Humboldt, Bidwell, Chapin and Lincoln parkways, Fillmore, Porter and Richmond avenues. The parkways are from 1,695 to 11,097 feet in length, and the beds are of stone and gravel, rolled hard and smooth and graded. They are each 100 feet wide. The Lake takes up forty-six and a half acres and was formed by damming Scajaquada Creek and by excavating. With its miniature islands, its bays and coves, the boat-house, well stocked with row-boats, and a float for the band, it is difficult to find a more romantic and picturesque spot. The popularity of the place is attested by the crowds of people to be seen there summer evenings. When the Parade Refectory (since burned) was first opened to the public fully 15,000 people, principally Germans, congregated there. The buildings were of wood and covered an area of 28,000 square feet. There were spacious verandas and pavilion wings, a roomy ball and concert room, saloon, dining halls, waiting rooms, etc. On the east end was a tower 138 feet high, from the observatory of which a fine view of the harbor, city and suburban district could be obtained. This costly and unique structure has been replaced by a less pretentious building which is used for similar purposes. It is a popular resort for the Germans, particularly on Sundays. Adjacent to the main park where the lake is situated is Forest Lawn Cemetery—solemn, grand and beautiful. The new State Insane Asylum, an imposing brown stone and brick structure rapidly nearing completion, is on the opposite side of the main park. About $1,500,000 have been expended on the parks, including the amount paid for the land.

The following interesting statistics will give some idea of the vast commerce of Buffalo.

ERRATUM.

On page 20, 8th line from bottom of second column, read "Grand total, bush. 44,101,689."

TRADE AND COMMERCE OF BUFFALO.

LAKE AND RAILROAD COMMERCE.

Summary.

The receipts of flour and grain in 1879 by lake at Buffalo aggregated 78,891,151 bushels, including flour reduced to its equivalent in wheat; the largest on record, excepting last year, when the figures were 84,090,939 bushels. The receipts by the steamer International were formerly added to the lake movement, but since the opening of the International bridge at Black Rock no statistics have been kept of the imports by the railroads at that point.

The business of the Lake Shore & Michigan Southern Railroad largely increased. The flour and grain movement this year was 45,201,300 bushels as compared with 33,508,300 bushels in 1878. The tonnage of the other articles enumerated shows very favorably when contrasted with last year's figures. The other railroads centering here do not make any reports by which the amount of their tonnage can be ascertained.

The aggregate receipts for 1879 by lake and the Lake Shore & Michigan Southern Railroad were 123,992,451 bushels of grain against 117,590,239 bushels in 1878, a gain of 6,393,212 bushels in favor of this year.

The growth of the grain trade of Buffalo is briefly shown by the following figures: In 1836 the receipts by lake were 1,239,351 bushels; in 1846, 13,366,168 bushels; in 1856, 25,753,967 bushels; in 1866, 53,388,087 bushels; in 1876, 50,074,648 bushels; in 1877, 65,190,291 bushels; in 1878, 84,046,052 bushels, and in 1879, 78,865,354 bushels. The aggregate receipts by lake of flour and grain from 1836 to 1879 inclusive were 1,526,266,253 bushels.

The lumber trade makes an excellent exhibit. It will be noticed that the imports and exports were generally larger, and prices correspondingly improved with the increased business. The stocks on hand are much larger than at this time last year, in anticipation of continued activity in the building trade.

The coal trade has made the greatest progress of any branch of commerce. The imports of anthracite aggregate 1,092,134 tons, bituminous 673,670 tons, and Blossburg 62,000 tons; total, 1,827,804 tons; an increase of about one-third over the imports of 1878. The exports by lake show a corresponding improvement. The manufacturing demand was very large, indicative of increased activity, and the domestic consumption was a little ahead of 1878.

The shipments of grain from the elevators by railroads connected therewith aggregate 16,308,526 bushels; for the corresponding period in 1878 the movement was 19,136,668 bushels; a falling off this year of 2,828,142 bushels.

The exports by lake for the past season include 580,646 tons of coal, 103,858 barrels of cement and plaster, 222,778 barrels and 26,372 tons of salt, and 525 tons of railroad iron; a gain over the business of 1878 of 249,474 tons of coal, 22,145 barrels of cement and plaster, and nearly 40,000 barrels of salt. The tonnage of other western-bound freight carried by propellers was the largest ever known.

The first arrival at this port by lake in 1879 was the steam barge Enterprise from Dresden, Ontario, Canada, on Thursday, April 24th. The Straits of Mackinaw were reported open the same day. Propellers commenced departing hence for upper lake ports on the 28th of April, but the ice blockade soon occurred at this end of Lake Erie, and free navigation was not secured until May the 18th.

Lake freights on grain from Chicago to Buffalo fluctuated considerably during the season; opening at 6c for wheat and 5½c for corn; gradually declining to 1⅞c and 1⅛c on June 7th; then advancing slowly to 8c and 7½c October 25th, and then declining again to 5½c and 5c respectively, the closing rates. Coal was carried from this port to Chicago and Milwaukee at rates ranging from 30c to $1 25 per ton. Probably the fair average for the season would be 60c per ton, as only $1 00 was paid for a few days in October and $1 00@1 25 at the close of November.

Railroad freights opened at 9½c for wheat and 9c for corn hence to New York; gradually declined to 5c and 4½c in July, and then slowly advanced to 12c and 11½c on and after November 10th.

Elevating and storage rates on grain opened at ⅝c per bushel, including ⅛c to vessel: on September 22d and after they were 1c per bushel, including ⅛c to vessel. On November 17th winter rates commenced. From the opening until September 22d, where no storage was had ⅛c per bushel was charged, including ⅛c to vessel.

The arrivals and departures of vessels in the district of Buffalo Creek for the season of 1879 were 8,447, aggregating 4,442,717 tonnage, a small decrease under 1878. The tonnage of vessels built and enrolled was 2,163.11, comprising the propeller New York; tug propellers T. H. Fulton, Minnie Maythem and M. M. Drake; steamers Josephine B. and Mamie Higgins; steam-yachts Musette, Parole, Fanchon and Elizabeth; the yacht Cygnet and the schooner Highland Maid. Twenty-four vessels changed hands by total transfer. The total tonnage of the port at the close of the fiscal year ending June 30th, was 211 vessels, of 97,734.46 tonnage, exclusive of canal boats other than steam, of which the custom house does not now keep a record. One hundred and nineteen vessels of all kinds are laid up here for the winter.

The number of vessels passing out of existence on the lakes in 1879 was 78, including 5 propellers, 4 sidewheel steamers, 1 steam barge, 6 tugs, 3 brigs, 8 barges, 9 scows, and 42 schooners, aggregating 18,531 tonnage, and valued at $316,075. The number of deaths was 208, an excess of 45 over 1878. The new vessels built were 19, of 13,918 tonnage and valued at $791,500. Net loss of tonnage, 4,013.

The amount of canal tolls collected at this port during the season aggregated $591,652, as compared with $628,439 in 1878, a decrease of $36,787 under 1879. It should be remembered however, that the canals in 1878 opened April 15th, and this year on May 8th, three weeks later. The number of boats cleared was 8,708; in 1878, 9047 ; a decrease of 339.

Canal navigation was interrupted on June 26th by the caving in of a culvert near Orangeport, and this accident with a break a few days later at another point delayed boats nearly fourteen days. The dryness of the season also caused frequent low water, and the ice from Rome eastward was troublesome on and after the 20th of November. All boats reached tidewater and the canal was closed officially on the 6th of December. The number of days of navigation was 212.

The exports by canal were 4,750 barrels of flour and 53,868,392 bushels of grain, or, reducing flour to grain, 53,892,142 bushels, as compared with 58,567,734 bushels in 1878. The principal products of the forest shipped were, 107,158,316 feet of lumber, 34,600,000 shingles, and 56,029,617 pounds of staves ; an increase of lumber and shingles, and a decrease of staves. Flaxseed was carried to the extent of 22,238,587 pounds, pig iron 923 tons, coal 28,284 tons, petroleum oil 55,435 barrels, and pork 2,131 barrels. The total tonnage was 1,830,843, of the value of $48,142,030.

The imports are well worthy of special notice, as they show the beneficial result of the free list on water transportation. The aggregate tonnage was 499,453, of the value of $43,554,105—nearly equal to the value of the exports. The principal articles imported were dried fruits, domestic woolens and cottons, pig iron, iron ore, salt, sugar, molasses, coffee, nails, iron and steel, railroad iron, crockery, coal and gypsum.

Canal freights from Buffalo to New York opened at 5½c for wheat and 5c for corn; gradually declined to 3⅜c and 3¼c for the week ending June 28th; then advanced to 9¼c and 8½c at the end of September and beginning of October; fluctuated to the highest point, 12c and 11c, on October 23d, 24th and 25th. During November 10@10½c and 8@9¼c respectively was obtained; closing at outside figures. Pine lumber varied from $2 25@4 00 per 1,000 feet, and staves from $1 00@2 50 per ton over tolls.

The receipts of flour and grain at tidewater from all the canals this year were 56,977,000 bushels as compared with 63,010,000 bushels in 1878.

The table of comparative prices of leading articles shows a large increase in the values of the articles enumerated, with but few exceptions, as compared with 1878—but our space will not allow of more particular mention.

The live stock trade during the year shows a falling off in cattle, sheep and hogs, but the business done, nevertheless, was very large, and is a material element conducive to the prosperity of the commercial interests of our city.

The receipts of flour and grain at the western lake ports of Chicago, Milwaukee, Toledo, Detroit, Cleveland and Duluth, from January 1st to December 27th, aggregate 228,042,847 bushels as compared with 225,259,114 bushels in 1878. The shipments for the same period from those places were 209,819,924 bushels in 1879, and 198,263,889 bushels in 1878. These figures show a gain for this year's cereal movement.

Comparative Imports by Lake.

The following table shows the imports of principal articles into this port by lake for the years 1877, 1878 and 1879:

	1877.	1878.	1879.
Ashes, casks	214	....	....
Ashes, tons	....	....	700
Ashes, leached, tons	235	....	....
Apples, bbls	8.2	....	....
Beef, bbls and tcs	506	....	....
Beans, bu	115	....	....
Beans, bbls	....	....	50
Barley, bu	1,652,566	1,375,184	610,710
Butter, lbs	5,000	949	....
Butter, pkgs	251	2,046	....
Bacon, bxs	589	6,035	....
Broomcorn, bls	1,385	953	103
Barrels, empty, no	4,705	....	....
Coal, tons	44,247	60,001	34,648
Cheese, bxs	125	....	....
Corn, bu	31,362,846	35,133,853	32,990,993
Cedar posts, no	24,012	8,209	16,730
Cornmeal, bbls	3,702	6,475	2,000
Copper, pkgs	11,623	7,804	12,685
Copper, tons	6,342	8,758	6,064
Copper, cakes and bars	12,616	8,781	17,791
Cattle, no	....	11	....
Eggs, doz	....	....	186
Eggs, pkgs	1,569	6,945	....
Fish, pkgs	21,153	8,617	5,120
Flour, bbls	693,044	971,980	897,105
Feed, sks	57,694	4,591	8,399
Grindstones, tons	195	65	....
Grindstones, no	288	331	....
Hides, no	4,593	5,140	....
Hides, tons	10	....	....
Hides, bdls	....	....	132
Horses, no	130	31	....
Hops, bales	....	178	9.52
Hams, tcs	619	1,002	....
Hoops, no	22,403.700	11,500,000	14,579,000
Hoop poles, no	19 1,620	200,000	....
Heading, bbls	6, 98	5,721	14,471
Iron ore, tons	1,997	14,737	25,580
Iron, pig, tons	5,650	5,447	8,431
Iron, tons	340	3,638	127
Iron, scrap, lbs	75,000	64,200	256,000
Iron, bdls	622	....	....
Iron, bars	3,639	....	....
Iron, plates	110	....	....
Lead, tons	5.7	147	46
Lead, pigs	51,805	35,719	6,965
Leather, rolls	230	538	40
Lard, lbs	770,000	....	249,920
Lard, tcs	53,400	88,278	81,831
Lard, pkgs	9,168	2,775	18,568
Lard, bbls	....	....	1,850

	1877.	1878.	1879.
Lumber, feet	141,572,169	176,322,464	202,443,612
Lath, pcs	6,392,200	3,535,000	4,644,000
Millfeed, lbs	407,000	....	....
Oats, bu	4,279,229	5,122,972	1,104,793
Oatmeal, bbls	1,557	7,518	2,500
Oatmeal, bags	....	....	4,443
Oil cake, pkgs	32,084	73,443	51,047
Oil cake, tons	504	245	379
Oil, bbls	3 337	3,340	480
Pickets, no	55,522	....	7,190
Pork, bbls	41,766	31,937	33,570
Peas, bu	57,450	44,887	25,797
Potatoes, bu	4,658	....	....
Pelts, bdls	3,236	823	754
Potash, tons	219	....	....
Plaster, bbls	1,000	....	....
Rye, bu	1,155,003	2,135,007	1,884,802
Sundries, pkgs	46,714	41,800	75,000
Silver ore, pkgs	3,540	....	536
Silver ore, tons	620	....	....
Seed, bags	265,993	351,716	293,742
Seed, bu	....	....	344,312
Stone, tons	814	....	59
Stone, cords	1,489	1,175	....
Salt, bbls	1,000	....	....
Staves, no	18,284,985	11,638,863	12,070,597
Stave bolts, cords	4,403	4,512	8,640
Shingles, no	54,251,000	66,273,000	59,793,700
Shooks, bdls	12,775	17,985	1,541
Shooks, no	....	....	767,000
Sheep, no	....	15	....
Tobacco, pkgs	2,766	3,358	4,143
Tallow, lbs	130,780	83,400	....
Tallow, pkgs	1,650	....	100
Tallow, bbls	590	278	411
Tallow, tcs	100	11,258	....
Ties, no	172,679	160,000	271,693
Whisky, bbls	27	51	....
Wool, bales	942	357	2,427
Wood, cords	2,516	1,084	1,400
Wheat, bu	23,284,405	35,419,136	37,788,501

AGGREGATE RECEIPTS OF FLOUR AND GRAIN.

	1877.	1878.	1879.
Flour, bbls	693,044	971,980	897,105
Wheat, bu	23,284,405	35,419,136	37,788,501
Corn, bu	31,362,846	35,133,835	32,990,993
Oats, bu	4,279,229	5,122,972	1,104,793
Barley, bu	1,652,568	1,375,184	610,740
Rye, bu	1,155,003	2,135,047	1,884,802
Peas, bu	57,450	44,887	25,797
Total grain, bu	61,794,521	79,231,039	74,405,626
Flour to wheat, bu	3,465,220	4,859,900	4,485,525
Grand total, bu	65,256,741	84,090,939	78,891,151

Receipts by Lake Shore & Michigan Southern Railroad.

The following table shows the principal receipts at Buffalo by the Lake Shore & Michigan Southern Railroad for the year ending December 31st, 1879, as compared with those of 1878 and 1877:

	1877.	1878.	1879.
Flour, bbls	1,100,000	947,400	1,187,700
Wheat, bu	4,219,900	8,243,200	12,916,700
Corn, bu	6,139,200	12,470,400	15,947,800
Oats, bu	3,669,100	5,721,300	8,869,10 1
Barley, bu	679,600	1,363,600	753,000
Rye, bu	815,600	972,800	776,200
Total grain, bu	15,523,400	28,771,300	39,262,800
Flour to wheat, bu	5,502,000	4,737,000	5,938,500
Grand total, bu	21,025,400	33,508,300	45,201,300

	1877.	1878.	1879.
Beef, bbls and tcs..	191,160	171,550	183,100
Butter, lbs.........	8,059,000	9,536,000	17,538,000
Bacon, lbs	27,140,000	25,560,000	24,540,000
Broomcorn, bales..	20,612	19,250	14,047
Coal, tons	156,958	98,916	70,808
Cattle, cars	24,746	30,925	36,146
Cheese, bxs	81,860	87,180	121,100
Cotton, bales......	110,090	73,550	119,572
Cornmeal, bbls	231,200	192,200	212,700
Eggs, pkgs.........	13,475	15,876	26,590
Fish, pkgs	22,054	20,949	26,420
Grindstones, no....	7,035	11,060	21,170
Hides, no	205,915	222,388	305,097
Horses, cars	660	648	1,061
Hops, bales	3,615	2,020	1,400
Hogs, cars.........	8,615	13,017	12,503
Hemp, bales	14,885	12,880	9,133
Hams, tcs..........	190,350	166,700	185,730
Iron, plates, uo ...	41,260	35,830	26,280
Iron, pig, tons	7,128	8,445	10,166
Leather, rolls......	10,400	9,570	12,702
Lard, lbs..........	14,880,000	21,990,000	20,270,000
Lumber, cars......	2,558	2,871	2,625
Oil cake, pkgs	153,010	97,470	156,630
Oil, refined, bbls...	1,198,630	1,698,750	1,156,745
Oil, crude, bbls	1,370,485	738,832	331,165
Pork, bbls	230,150	201,900	238,150
Pelts, bdls	18,000	13,980	14,370
Seed, bags	47,760	35,511	41,300
Stones, tons.......	4,590	4,964	8,551
Staves, cars.......	426	398	440
Sheep, cars	2,157	2,935	2,907
Tobacco, pkgs.....	27,370	21,810	27,910
Tobacco, hhds .	6,525	5,251	5,623
Tallow,bbls or pkgs	7,779	8,445	7,080
Tanbark, cars......	785	623	455
Whisky, bbls	60,670	56,610	73,550
Wool, bales	22,934	20,470	27,755

Of the above receipts for 1877, 1878 and 1879 the following were for this city:

	1877.	1878.	1879.
Flour, bbls.........	31,300	34,500	31,400
Wheat, bu	58,700	16,200	126,200
Corn, bu	224,000	300,000	136,800
Oats, bu...........	81,900	100,800	130,000
Barley, bu	14,400	92,000	22,000
Rye, bu	6,000	4,800	2,400
Hides, no	67,075	68,278	103,182
Fish, pkgs	4,264	6,361	7,585
Lumber, cars......	798	1,072	1,145
Oil, refined, bbls...	48,626	45,910	36,630
Oil, crude, bbls....	8,070	1,275	905
Coal, tons.........	111,908	87,954	53,118

Flour and Grain Receipts by Lake and the Lake Shore & Michigan Southern Railroad.

The following statement shows the receipts of flour and grain by Lake and the Lake Shore & Michigan Southern Railroad in 1877, 1878 and 1879:

	1877.	1878.	1879.
Flour, bbls.........	1,793,444	1,919,380	2,084,805
Wheat, bu	27,504,305	43,662,336	50,705,201
Corn, bu	37,502,066	47,604,253	48,938,793
Oats, bu...........	7,939,329	10,844,272	9,973,893
Barley, bu	2,332,168	2,738,784	1,363,740
Rye, bu	1,970,603	3,107,807	2,661,002
Peas, bu..........	57,450	44,887	25,797
Total, bu........	77,305,921	108,002,339	113,668,426
Flour to wheat, bu.	8,967,220	9,596,900	10,424,025
Grand total, bu ..	87,273,141	117,599,239	123,992,451

NOTE.—No returns made of the traffic over the International bridge in 1877, 1878 and 1879. The receipts would be largely increased if these figures could be given.

Grain Trade of Buffalo for Forty-four Years.

The following statement shows the grain trade of Buffalo for forty-four years (the receipts by the Lake Shore Railroad not included):

Years.	Flour, bbls.	Wheat, bu.	Corn, bu.
1836	139.178	804,000	204,355
1837	126,805	430,350	94,490
1838	277,620	943.117	34,148
1839	294,125	1,117,262	----
1840	597,142	1,004,561	71,337
1841	730,040	1,635,000	201,031
1842	734,408	1,555,420	1454,530
1843	917,517	1,827,241	223,966
1844	915,030	2,174,500	137,978
1845	746,750	1,770,740	54,200
1846	1,374,529	4,744,184	1,455,258
1847	1,857,000	6,489,100	2,562,800
1848	1,249,000	4,520,117	2,298,000
1849	1,207,435	4,943,978	3,321,651
1850	1,103,039	8,681,347	2,503,378
1851	1,258,224	4,167,121	5,988,775
1852	1,299,213	5,549,748	5,136,718
1853	975,557	5,420,043	8,065,793
1854	739,756	3,510,782	10,108,983
1845	986,761	8,022,126	9,711,430
1856	1,126,048	8,465,691	9,633,277
1857	845,953	8,334,179	5,713,611
1858	1,536,109	10,971,550	6,621,663
1859	1,420,333	9,284,652	3,113,653
1860	1,122,335	18,502,645	11,386,217
1861	2,159,591	27,105,219	21,034,657
1862	2,846,522	30,435,531	24,388,627
1863	2,978,089	21,240,848	20,086,9 2
1864	2,028,520	17,677,549	10,478,081
1865	1,788,393	13,437 588	19,840 901
1866	1,313,543	10,479,694	27,894,798
1867	1,440,056	11,879,685	17,873,658
1868	1,502,781	12,555,215	16,804,067
1869	1,598,487	19,228,516	11,549,493
1870	1,470,391	20,556,722	9,410,128
1871	1,278,077	22,606,217	26,110,769
1872	762,502	14,304,942	31,643,187
1873	1 259,205	30,618,312	26,550,828
1874	1,693,585	29,778,512	21,971,513
1875	1,810,402	32,907,686	12,593,691
1876	807,210	19,324 612	20 939,853
1877*	693,044	23,284,405	33,362,866
1878*	971,980	35,419,136	35,133,8 3
1879*	897,105	37,788,501	32,990,903

	Oats, bu	Barley, bu.	Rye, bu.
1836	28,640	4,876	1,500
1837	2,553	....	3,267
1838	6,577	....	909
1839	....	....	....
1840	....	....	....
1841	14,144	....	2,150
1842	....	4,710	1,288
1843	2,489	....	1,332
1844	18,017	16,7	456
1845	23,300	....	....
1846	218,300	47,530	23,250
1847	446,000	....	70,787
1848	560,000	6	17,859
1849	362,384	....	....
1850	357,580	3,600	....
1851	1,140,340	142,773	10,652
1852	2,296,231	497,913	112,251
1853	1,580,655	401,098	107,152
1854	4,401,739	818,885	177,066
1855	2,083,222	62,304	299,591
1856	1,733,884	46 327	245,810
1857	1,214,760	37,844	48,586
1858	2,275,231	308,371	125,214
1859	894,502	36,580	124,633
1860	1 209,594	202,158	80,822
1861	1,797,905	313,757	337 784
1862	2 624,932	423,124	791,564
1863	7,322,187	641,449	422,300
1864	11,032,637	465,057	633,727
1870	8,484,799	820,508	877,676
1871	10,227,472	1,606,384	1,245,485

	Oats, bu.	Barley, bu.	Rye, bu.
1872...	10,933,166	1,802,598	1,010,603
1873...	11,492,474	637,124	947,323
1865...	5,459,347	651,339	126,093
1866...	6.846,983	1,821,104	626,154
1867...	9,006,109	1,906,923	1,095,039
1886...	6,050,045	3,088,925	301,809
1861...	5,972,846	1,232,507	916,947
1874...	5,896,741	1,154,948	167,301
1875...	8,494,124	9'6,889	222,126
1876...	2,397,257	2,615,084	761,795
1877*...	4,279,249	1,652,568	1,155,003
1878*...	5,122,972	1,375,184	2,135,0 7
1879*...	1,104,795	616,740	1,864,802

GRAIN INCLUDING FLOUR AS GRAIN.

Years.	Grain, bush.	Grain, including flour, bush.
1836	548,461	1,239,351
1837	550,660	1,184,685
1838	974,751	2,587,887
1839	1,117,262	2,362,851
1840	1,075,888	4,061,508
1841	1,852,325	5,592,525
1842	2,015,928	5,687,468
1843	2,055,025	6,642,610
1844	2,335,568	6,910,718
1845	1,848,040	5,581,790
1846	6,491,522	13,366,167
1847	9,868,187	19,153,187
1848	7,396,012	14,641,018
1849	8,628,013	14,665,189
1850	6,618,004	12,059,551
1851	11,449,661	17,740,584
1852	13,392,937	20,390,506
1853	11,078,741	15,956,525
1854	18,553,455	22,252,288
1855	19,788,478	24,472,277
1856	20,123,667	25,753,965
1857	15,348,930	19,578,090
1858	20,202,444	26,812,982
1859	14,429,060	21,530,722
1860	31,411,440	37,053,115
1861	50,062,646	61,460,601
1862	58,642,314	72,872,454
1863	49,845,005	64,735,510
1864	41,044,496	51,177,146
1865	42,473,223	51,415,388
1866	51,820,342	53,388,087
1867	43,460,780	50,700,060
1868	42,436,204	49,949,856
1869	37,014,728	45,007,163
1870	39,261,141	46,613,086
1871	60,765,357	67,155,742
1872	58,417,822	62,260,332
1873	67,340,570	73,636,595
1874	61,562,627	70 0 0 552
1875	65,194,716	74,246,726
1876	46,038,598	50,074,648
1877*	61,734,071	65,199,291
1878*	79,1,6,152	84,046,052
1879*	74,379,829	78,865,354

COMPARED BY DECADES.

Years.	Grain, bush.	Grain, including flour, bush.
1836	548 461	1,239,351
1846	6,491,522	13,366,167
1856	20,123,667	25,753,967
1866	51,820,342	53,388,087
1876	46,038,598	50,074,648

AGGREGATE RECEIPTS COMPARED.

Decades.	Grain, bush.	Grain, including flour, bush.
1836 to 1845—10 years..	14,368,908	41,851,483
1846 to 1855—10 years...	113,760,005	174,717,437
1856 to 1865—10 years...	344,213,324	432,390,318
1866 to 1875—10 years...	526,976,775	597 121 670
1876	46,038,598	50 074,648
1877*	61,734 071	65,199,291

Decades.	Grain, bush.	Grain, including Flour, bush.
1878*	79,176,152	84 046,052
1879*	74,379,829	78,865,354
Total 44 years ..	1,262,435,711	1,526,266,253

*Canadian receipts through Custom-house not included in 1877, 1878 and 1879.

Lumber Trade of Buffalo.

The following table shows the receipts and shipments of lumber, etc., for three years:

IMPORTS BY CANAL.

	1877.	1878.	1879.
Lumber, feet......	328.071	888,145	1,703,849
Timber, cubic feet.	8,225	5,016	82,862
Shingles, no........	177,000	10,000	30,000

EXPORTS BY CANAL.

Lumber, feet.......	79,782,686	95,310,685	107,158,316
Staves, lbs	82,359,650	77,482,200	56,029,617
Shingles, no........	30,542,000	29,283,000	34,600,000

IMPORTS BY LAKE.

Heading, bbls......	6,198	5,721	14,471
Hoops, no...........	22,463,700	11,500,000	14.579,000
Hoop poles, no......	190,620	2'0,000	....
Lumber, feet	141,572,469	176,312,464	202,443,612
Lath, pieces	6,392,200	3,545,000	4,644,000
Railroad ties, no...	172,079	160,000	271,693
Staves, no.........	18,284,885	11,638,868	12,070,597
Stave bolts, cords..	4,403	4,512	8,610
Shingles, no........	54,254,000	66,273,000	59,793,700
Shooks, bundles ...	12,775	17,985	1,541
Pickets, no.........	55,522	....	7,190
Cedar posts, no	24,012	8,209	16,730

OTHER IMPORTS BY RAILROADS AND TEAMS.*

Lumber, feet	75,000,000	90,000,000	90,00,000

*Partly estimated.

AVERAGE PRICES.

The prices at the yards during 1879 were about as follows, per 1,000 feet:

Basswood ...$14 00@20 00	Chestnut....$22 00@36 00
Pine .... 8 00@40 00	Walnut..... 30 00@80 00
Ash .... 14 00@35 00	Maple....... 18 00@32 00
Whitewood . 14 00@35 00	Hickory .... 25 00@45 00
Oak .... 19 00@37 00	Lath, per M. 1 65@ 2 00
Cherry ..... 32 00@45 00	Shingles, do. 1 80@ 3 25

Coal Trade of Buffalo.

The anthracite and bituminous coal trade of this city is shown by the following figures:

IMPORTS BY CANAL.

	1877.	1878.	1879.
Anthracite, tons	208,609	115,102	92,134
Blossburg, tons.........	10,000	3,353	2,000

EXPORTS BY CANAL.

Bituminous, tons	29,250	30,820	28,290

IMPORTS BY LAKE.

Bituminous, tons	44,247	50,004	56,648

EXPORTS BY LAKE.

Anthracite, tons	405,074	306,172	550,646
Blossburg, tons.........	50,000	25,000	30,000

IMPORTS BY RAILROADS.*

Anthracite, tons	550,000	660,000	1,050,000
Bituminous, tons	214,200	425,973	637,022
Blossburg, tons	50,000	45,000	60,000

EXPORTS BY RAILROADS.

No estimate to hand of the movement in detail.

RECAPITULATION.

Total imports, Anthra-
cite, tons 750,609   775,162   1,092,134
Do., Bituminous, tons ..258,447   474,974   673,670
Do. Blossburg, tons 60,000   23,353   62,000
Total exports, Bitumi-
nous 29,250   39,820   28,290
Do., Anthracite, tons...405,074   306,172   550,646
Do., Blossburg, tons.... 50,000   25,000   30,000
*Partly estimated.

The retail prices of anthracite per 2,000 pounds, delivered in city limits, during the year were as follows:

	Grate.	Egg.	Stove.	Nut.	Bloss-burg.
1879.					
Jan'y 1.......	$5 15	$5 25	$5 50	$5 00	$4 00
April 19.......	3 75	3 75	4 00	3 75	4 00
May 24.......	3 25	3 25	3 50	3 50	3 50
May 3	3 50	3 50	3 75	3 75	3 50
Oct. 13.......	3 90	3 90	4 00	4 00	3 50
Oct. 20	4 10	4 10	4 20	4 20	3 50
Nov. 1.......	4 35	4 35	4 45	4 60	3 50
Dec. 1.......	4 65	4 65	4 85	5 10	3 75
Dec. 31.......	4 65	4 65	4 85	5 10	3 75

The range of prices during 1879 for bituminous, delivered to manufactories, gas works, propeller lines, etc., were from $2 10 to $4 00 per ton, according to description. The price at retail varied from $4 00 to $6 00 delivered per ton, according to quality, for family use.

About 185,000 tons of anthracite and bituminous coal were consumed by families in this city during 1879.

Comparative Prices of Leading Articles.

The following statement shows the approximate ruling rates of the various articles enumerated at Buffalo December 30, 1879, and the corresponding periods in 1878 and 1877:

Flour, bbl—	1877.	1878.	1879.
City gr. sp. No. 1.	$6 25@ 6 75	$5 00@ 5 50	$6 75@ 7 25
City gr. sp. No. 2.	5 25@ 5 75	3 75@ 4 25	5 50@ 6 25
City gr'd amber.	7 00@ 7 50	5 25@ 5 75	7 25@ 7 75
City gr'd white .	7 25@ 7 75	5 50@ 6 00	7 50@ 8 00
C. g. new proc's.	8 50@ 9 50	7 25@ 7 75	8 25@ 9 00
Western spring .	6 00@ 6 75	4 25@ 5 25	6 00@ 7 50
Western bakers'	6 50@ 7 00	4 50@ 6 00	7 00@ 7 50
Western amber.	7 00@ 7 50	4 75@ 5 25	7 50@ 8 00
Western white..	7 25@ 7 75	5 25@ 6 00	7 75@ 8 25
Western new pr.	8 50@ 9 00	7 00@ 8 00	8 75@ 9 75
Rye	4 00@ 4 50	3 25@ 3 50	5 50@ 6 00
Buckwheat, cwt	2 65@ 3 00	2 00@ 2 25	3 00@ 3 00
Wheat, bush—			
No. 1 spring	1 27	1 00	......
No. 2 spring.....	1 23	95	......
No. 1 Duluth sp.	1 25	1 07	1 43
No.1 h'dDu'th sp	——	——	1 45
Red and amber.	1 32@ 1 38	95@ 1 00	1 38@ 1 45
White ...	1 38@ 1 41	90@ 1 03	1 40@ 1 47
Corn, bush—			
No. 2 Western..	53@ 53½	40½@ 41	53½
Oats, bu, West'n	34@ 31	26@ 29	45
Rye, bu, do .	70@ 74	52½	90
Barley, bush—			
West. and Can..	70 @ 85	61@ 1 10	70@ 90
State, 2 & 4 r'w'd	50@ 73	75@ 92	65@ 80
Barley mа't,bu.	75@ 1 15	1 10@ 1 30	1 05@ 1 25
Peas. bu,(free of			
du'y mada.	1 10@ 1 20	80@ 90	95@ 1 00
Beans, bu.......	1 60@ 2 15	1 50@ 1 70	1 50
Seed, clover, bu.	4 75@ 5 50	4 50@ 5 25	5 50@ 5 75
Seed, timothy,bu	1 40@ 1 60	1 35@ 1 45	2 30
Mill feed, ton—			
Coarse	16 00 11 00	@ 12 00 16 00@ 17 00	
Fine	17 00 13 00	@ 14 00 16 00@ 17 00	
Finished	20 00 13 00	@ 14 00 17 00 @ 18 00	

Flour, bbl—	1877.	1878.	1879.
Rye	17 00@19 00	14 00@15 00	18 00@19 00
Cornmeal, 100 lb	1 05@ 1 20	80@ 90	1 05@ 1 15
Oatmeal, bbl ...	5 00@ 7 00	4 00@ 6 50	6 00@ 7 00
Mess pork, bbl—			
Heavy	12 00@12 50	8 50@ 9 00	13 50
Short cut	12 00@12 50	9 00@ 9 50	13 50
Lard, lb	8@ 9	6½@ 6¾	8@ 8½
Dres'd hogs, cwt	4 50 @ 4 75	2 75@ 3 50	6 00
Highwines, gal.	1 09@ 1 10	1 07@ 1 08	1 12
Potatoes, bu	35@ 50	60@ 80	40@ 45
Butter, lb.......	14 @ 25	12 @ 20	18@ 27
Cheese,dairy,lb.	12	7@ 8	11
Do., factory, lb..	13@ 13½	9 @ 9½	12
Hops, lbs.......	11@ 13	8 @ 11	30@ 35
Eggs, doz.	21@ 23	23 @ 25	2 @ 23
Cranberries, bbl	7 00@ 8 00	6 25@ 7 50	8 00
Apples,dried,lb.	5½@ 7	3½@ 5	7@ 8
Do., green, bbl..	2 25@ 3 25	1 25@ 2 00	1 75@ 2 50
Oranges, case ..	7 00 @ 7 50	5 00@ 6 00	5 00@ 5 50
Lemons, box.....	3 50@ 4 00	3 00@ 5 00	4 00
Salt, coarse, bbl.	1 00	80	1 40
Salt, fine, bbl .	95	85	1 40
Coal, Anthracite, retail price, delivered, ton—			
Grate............	5 20	5 15	4 65
Egg	5 20	5 25	4 35
Chestnut.......	5 35	5 00	5 10
Stove	5 45	5 50	4 85
Coal,bituminous	5 50@ 6 50	5 00@ 5 50	6 00
Hides, green, lb.	8@ 9	8½@ 10½	9½@ 10
Do., cured	12@ 14	14@ 18	16@ 17
Leather, lb—			
Best sl'ght'd sole	31	26	31
No. 2 do........	29	21	29
Cement, bbl.....	1 00 @ 1 25	1 15@ 1 25	80@ 1 00
Refined Petroleum, gallon, fire test—			
112 @ 120°......	12½@ 16	10	8@ 9
Pease's Pr'm oil	30@ 35	35	35
Pease's H'dlight	25	25	25
Lard Oil—			
Extra winter,gal	75 @ 80	60	60
Do., No. 1, do ..	65@ 70	55	58
Linseed oil, raw.	55	60	75
Do., boiled, gal.	62	65	78
W. V. oil, black,			
gallon	25	23	23
Do., gal., in bbl	30	25	25
Sperm oil, gal ..	1 50	1 25	1 00
Fish, half bbl—			
White...........	4 25 @ 4 33	3 40@ 3 50	5 00@ 5 50
Trout	3 25@ 3 38	3 00	4 00@ 4 25
Siscoes	3 00	1 60	3 00@ 3 25
Codfish, George's			
Bank, cwt.....	5 25@ 5 75	5 00	5 00@ 5 50
Halibut, cwt....	1 00	6 00	11 00
Mackerel, kit...	1 75@ 2 30	1 90@ 2 40	1 20@ 3 75
Do., bbl	15 00 a 22 00	12 00 a 18 00	11 00 a 22 00
St'ling Exch'ge.	4 82@ 4 85	4 82@ 4 87	4 81@ 4 84
Gold............	1 02¾	1 00	1 00

Exports from Elevators by Erie and Central Railroads.

The following statement shows the exports of grain from the elevators of this city by the Erie and Central railroads for the months of—

1879.	Wheat, bu.	Corn, bu.	Oats, bu.	Barley, bu.	Rye, bu.
January ..	334,350	19,005	23,879	9,093	....
February .	143,542	....	....	....	....
March	336,131	....	43,000	1,650	....
April	196,151	1,400	....	1,981	....
May	507,370	482,782	4,800	6,500	....
June......	345,142	518,354	1,400	25,000	....
July	555,015	1,398,882	72,382	....	12,029
August ...	1,759,716	1,319,718	....	....	46,607
Sept'mber.	1,505,889	849,732	42,000	....	....
October...	1,142,542	1,324,315	850	30,463	18,195
Nov'mber.	776,882	865,728	....	2,150	5,000
Dec'mber.	85 ,099	550,011	....	17,116	....
Total ...	8,575,129	7,369,007	188,329	94,230	81,831

	Wheat, bu.	Corn, bu.	Oats, bu.	Barley, bu.	Rye, bu.
Total 1878	9,173,439	9,300,650	254,057	185,212	223,310
Total 1877	9,323,318	3,854,034	620,009	348,082	90,332
Total 1876	5,984,722	6,581,929	715,049	112,741	278,291
Total 1875	6,198,393	6,433,717	1,091,327	60,437	16,786
Total 1874	4,658,080	5,209,202	1,318,097	191,277	10,318

Grand total, bushels, 1874	11,386,974
" " 1875	14,800,660
" " 1876	13,672,732
" " 1877	14,235,805
" " 1878	19,136,668
" " 1879	16,308,526
Decrease 1879 under 1878, bushels	2,828,142

Lake Exports.

The following statement, collated from the clearances issued during the season of navigation at the Custom-house of this port, shows the exports of the articles named during the seasons of navigation in 1877, 1878 and 1879 westward by lake:

	1877.	1878.	1879.
Coal, tons	455,074	331,172	580,646
Cement and plaster, bbls.	113,623	81,113	103,858
Salt, bbls	321,615	247,452	222,778
Salt, tons	7,235	18,767	26,372
Railroad iron, tons	1,509	283	525
Railroad iron, bars	....	2,170	....
Pig iron, tons	Not reported.		

Lake Freights from Buffalo to Chicago on Coal.

The following statement shows the ruling rates of freight on coal per ton, free, by sail vessels from Buffalo to Chicago during the season of 1879:

1879.	Coal, ton.	1879.	Coal, ton.
April 28	$0 40	Sept. 22	$0 70
May 7	30	Sept. 24	75
June 4	35	Oct. 6	85
June 20	40	Oct. 14	90
June 23	45	Oct. 15	1 00
July 1	50	Oct. 22	85
Aug. 6	40	Oct. 25	90
Aug. 25	50	Oct. 27	75
Sept. 11	55	Nov. 17	1 00
Sept. 15	60	Nov. 18	1 25

The dates given are the days on which the changes were made.

Lake Freights from Chicago to Buffalo on Wheat and Corn.

The following statement shows the ruling rates of lake freights on wheat and corn from Chicago to Buffalo, by sail vessels, on the dates specified in 1879:

1879.	Wheat, bu.	Corn, bu.	1879.	Wheat, bu.	Corn, bu.
April 17 noml.	6	5½	Aug. 9	5	4¾
April 26	4½	4	Aug. 16	5½	5
May 2	3¼	3	Aug. 23	5	4½
May 9	3½	3	Aug. 30	5¼	4½
May 12	3	2¾	Sept. 6	5	4½
May 17	3½	3	Sept. 13	5	4½
May 21	2¾	2½	Sept. 20	5	4½
May 31	2½	2¼	Sept. 27	6½	6
June 7	1¾	1½	Oct. 4	6½	6
June 14	2	1⅞	Oct. 11	7½	7
June 21	2	1¾	Oct. 18	8½	7¾
June 28	2	1¾	Oct. 25	8	7½
July 5	2¼	2	Nov. 1	7½	7
July 12	2¼	2	Nov. 8	7½	7
July 19	2¼	2	Nov. 15	6½	6
July 26	3¼	3	Nov. 22	5½	5
Aug. 2	4¼	4	Nov. 25	5½	5

Railroad Freights from Buffalo to New York on Wheat and Corn.

The following statement shows the *nominal* rates of freight on wheat and corn by railroad from Buffalo to New York during the year 1879:

1879.	Wheat, bu.	Corn, bu.
January 1 to May 4	9½	9
May 5 to May 15	7	6½
May 16 to May 28	6½	6
May 29 to July 25	5	4½
July 26 to July 29	5½	5
July 30 to August 10	6	5½
August 11 to August 15	7	6½
August 16 to August 25	8	7½
August 26 to October 12	9	8½
October 13 to November 9	10½	10
November 10 to December 31	12	11½

Elevating and Storage Rates at Buffalo.

The following shows the current rates as published by the Western Elevating Company, during the days specified in 1879:

JANUARY 1 to APRIL 30.—Winter storage, which commenced November 18, 1878, was: Elevating, including ten days' storage, one cent per bushel; seven-eighths of one cent to the grain and one-eighth of one cent to the vessel. Storage, each succeeding ten days or parts thereof, one-quarter of one cent per bushel. On grain in store on that date or after, the charge for winter storage will be one-quarter of one cent per bushel for each ten days or parts thereof until such charge (accumulated after November 18, 1878) shall amount to two cents per bushel; then the grain shall be free of storage until five days after the opening of canal navigation in 1879.

MAY 1 to SEPTEMBER 21.—For elevating and transferring half of one cent per bushel; for elevating, transferring and storing for first five days or parts thereof, five-eighths of one cent per bushel; for storage, each succeeding ten days, or parts thereof, in addition, one-quarter of a cent per bushel. The vessel pays, in addition to the above, one-eighth of one cent per bushel.

SEPTEMBER 22 to NOVEMBER 16.—For elevating and transferring, including five days' storage, seven-eighths of one cent per bushel. Storage, each succeeding ten days or parts thereof, one-quarter of a cent. The vessel pays, in addition to the above, per bushel, one-eighth of a cent.

NOVEMBER 17.—The following card was issued: "Elevating, including ten days' storage, seven-eighths of one cent per bushel. Storage, each succeeding ten days or parts thereof, one-quarter of one cent per bushel. The vessel pays, in addition to the above, per bushel, one-eighth cent. On all grain in store on that date or after, the charge for winter storage will be one-quarter cent per bushel for each ten days or parts thereof, until such charge (accumulated after November 17th, 1879,) shall amount to two cents per bushel; then the grain shall be free of storage until five days after the opening of canal navigation in 1880."

Arrivals and Clearances for the Season of Navigation.

The following is a statement of the arrivals and clearances by lake of vessels of all kinds, with the total tonnage, at and from this port during the season of 1879:

COASTWISE ARRIVALS.

	No.	Tons.
May	378	225,227
June	400	251,054
July	487	290,026
August	626	354,283
September	659	363,214
October	713	295,056
November	355	237,853
December	68	60,875
Total	3,686	2,077,558

COASTWISE CLEARANCES.

	No.	Tons.
April	24	17,883
May	469	281,932
June	426	246,119
July	4·6	263,915
August	625	352,360
September	658	355,213
October	706	346,304
November	357	342,761
December	28	27,570
Total	3,788	2,204,158

AMERICAN FOREIGN ARRIVALS.

	No.	Tons.
May	4	551
June	11	953
July	16	2,925
August	17	3,197
September	11	2,045
October	15	1,796
November	8	603
December	6	478
Total	88	12,848

AMERICAN FOREIGN CLEARANCES.

	No.	Tons.
May	5	721
June	11	879
July	18	2,820
August	17	3,677
September	9	1,103
October	13	1,451
November	9	696
December	2	71
Total	84	11,718

FOREIGN ARRIVALS.

	No.	Tons.
March	1	31
April	5	261
May	52	9,845
June	73	11,901
July	71	11,403
August	55	10,563
September	45	7,401
October	64	10,746
November	47	8,124
December	3	725
Total	410	71,000

FOREIGN CLEARANCES.

	No.	Tons.
March	1	31
April	8	968
May	59	7,872
June	70	11,262
July	73	11,901
August	53	8,919
September	43	7,390

	No.	Tons.
October	55	7,924
November	46	8,795
December	2	534
Total	390	65,435

Lake Arrivals and Departures.

The following is a summary statement of the arrivals and departures of vessels, with their tonnage, in the District of Buffalo Creek, for the season of 1879; also a comparative statement showing the aggregate figures for twenty-eight years:

ARRIVALS.

	No. vessels.	Tonnage.
Vessels in coastwise trade	3,686	2,077,558
Foreign vessels	504	83,848
Totals, 1879	4,190	2,161,406
Totals, 878	4,382	2,364,031
Decrease, 1879	192	202,505

DEPARTURES.

	No. vessels.	Tonnage.
Vessels in coastwise trade	3,788	2,204,158
Foreign vessels	474	77,153
Totals, 1879	4,257	2,281,311
Totals, 1878	4,361	2,304,657
Decrease, 1879	104	23,346

COMPARATIVE TABLE FOR TWENTY-EIGHT YEARS.

	No. vessels.	Tonnage.	Men.
1852	9,441	3,062,247	127,491
1853	8,298	3,252,978	128,112
1854	8,942	3,990,284	120,838
1855	9,211	3,380,233	114,575
1856	8,128	3,018,589	112,051
1857	7,581	3,226,806	132,183
1858	8,838	3,329,246	86,887
1859	10,521	5,952,626	1 8,119
1860	11,517	4,710,175	120,497
1861	13,866	5,963,896	144,173
1862	16,390	6,689,191	166,133
1863	15,376	6,757,903	157,415
1864	14,105	6,891,318	148,161
1865	13,746	7,032,593	145,074
1866	13,682	6,954,850	141,622
1867	12,826	5,806,960	129,300
1868	11,812	4,234,339	116,320
1869	10,201	4,007,496	103,673
1870	10,625	4,157,793	105,798
1871	10,891	4,852,641	115,209
1872	10,303	4,678,058	106,291
1873	9,959	4,886,733	107,785
1874	7,447	3,641,019	82,862
1875	6,278	3,250,839	71,392
1876	4,624	2,757,986	55,459
1877	6,785	3,530,219	73,893
1878	8,743	4,668,688	No report
1879	8,417	4,442,717	"

Opening and Closing of Navigation.

Statement showing the dates at which navigation opened and closed at Buffalo for ten years:

Year.	Lake opened.	Canal opened.	Canal closed.	No. days open.
1870	April 16	May 10	Dec. 8	212
1871	April 1	April 24	Nov. 28	220
1872	May 6	May 13	Nov. 30	202
1873	April 29	May 15	Nov. 24*	208
1874	April 18	May 5	Dec. 5	215
1875	May 12	May 18	Nov. 30	197
1876	May 4	May 4	Dec. 1	209

17

Lake opened.	Canal opened.	No. Days Canal closed.	Canal open.
1877	April 17	May 8	Dec. 7	213
1878 .... M'ch 16	April 15	Dec. 7	237
1879 ....April 24	May 8	Dec. 6	212

*Navigation unimpeded here for several days after this date, but no shipments made except to Lockport; navigation closed by ice east of Rome about the 24th; re-opened from December 12th to 25th, inclusive.

NOTE.—The Welland Canal opened May 5th and closed December 5th. The Straits of Mackinac opened April 22 t.

Vessels Built and Enrolled.

The following is a list of vessels built and enrolled and licensed in the District of Buffalo Creek, N. Y., during the year 1879:

	Tonnage.
Tug Propeller T. H. Fulton	13.74
Steam Yacht Musette	10.10
Steamer Josephine B	68.49
Tug Propeller Minnie Maythem	12.78
Steam Yacht Parole	5.96
Tug Propeller M. M. Drake	13.31
Steam Yacht Fanchon	16.23
Steamer Mamie Higgins	77.49
Propeller New York	1,921.68
Steam Yacht Elizabeth	13.32
Schooner Highland Maid	14.24
Sloop Yacht Cygnet	15.77
Total tonnage, 1879	2,183.11
Total tonnage, 1878	3,685.12
Total tonnage, 1877	1,844.03

Decrease of tonnage in 1879 under 1878, 1,502.01

The vessels built but not enrolled during the years 1878 and 1879 were not reported at the Custom-house.

Tonnage of Vessels.

The tonnage of the port of Buffalo, N. Y., for the fiscal year ending June 30, 1879, is shown by the following statement:

SAIL VESSELS.

Schooners	72	Barks	2
Total			74
Total tonnage			36,922.90

STEAM VESSELS.

Iron steamers.	5	Iron yachts	2
Total			7
Total tonnage			6,381.08
Tug propellers.	46	Propellers	47
Steam yachts..	13	Sidewheel st'r.	1
St'm canal boat	1		
Total			108
Total tonnage			49,227.16

BARGES.

Barges	22
Total tonnage	5,203.32
Grand total 1879	211 vessels; tonnage 97,731.16
Grand total 1878	223 vessels; tonnage 98,004.31

Dec. 1879 under 1878.. 12 vessels; tonnage 359.85

NOTE.—No figures kept of the tonnage of canal boats excepting those propelled by steam power.

Transfer of Vessels.

The following statement shows the number and description of the vessels changing owners by entire transfer at Buffalo during the year 1879:

Schooners	7	Tugs	6
Propellers	3	Yachts	2
Barges	6		—
Total transfers, 1879			24
Total transfers, 1878			29

Decrease 1879 under 1878 5

Comparative Receipts and Shipments and Cereal Crop Movement at Lake Ports.

COMPARATIVE RECEIPTS AT SIX WESTERN LAKE PORTS—Chicago, Milwaukee, Toledo, Detroit, Cleveland and Duluth, from January 1 to December 31:

	1879.	1878.	1877.
Flour, bbls	6,569,490	6,246,084	5,377,222
Wheat, bu	86,139,146	81,632,418	46,904,313
Corn, bu	74,980,433	76,432,177	61,920,421
Oats, bu	21,403,887	23,265,194	17,884,510
Barley, bu	9,306,150	9,381,857	6,889,096
Rye, bu	3,365,831	3,294,048	2,116,649
Total grain, bu.	195,195,397	194,028,694	135,714,659
Flour to wheat, bu	32,847,450	31,230,420	26,886,110
Grand total, bu.	228,042,847	225,259,114	162,600,769

COMPARATIVE SHIPMENTS AT SIX WESTERN LAKE PORTS—Chicago, Milwaukee, Toledo, Detroit, Cleveland and Duluth, from January 1 to December 31:

	1879.	1878.	1877.
Flour, bbls	6,767,279	6,417,392	5,514,887
Wheat, bu	75,636,746	60,419,248	44,390,378
Corn, bu	74,010,330	68,467,98	59,792,308
Oats, bu	16,660,26.6	19,006,719	15,736,102
Barley, bu	6,880,019	6,137,168	6,169,856
Rye, bu	3,416,228	2,995,567	1,791,415
Total grain, bu.	175,983,529	166,025,929	127,820,059
Flour to wheat, bu	33,836,395	32,236,960	27,574,435
Grand total, bu.	209,819,924	198,262,889	155,394,494

CEREAL CROP MOVEMENT AT LAKE PORTS COMPARED—Including receipts at Chicago, Milwaukee, Toledo, Detroit, Cleveland and Duluth, from August 1 to December 31, in the years named:

	1879.	1878.	1877.
Flour, bbls	2,852,865	2,657,504	1,988,428
Wheat, bu	51,354,649	47,385,739	38,930,163
Corn, bu	33,441,065	34,508,216	28,464,602
Oats, bu	9,709,588	12,163,341	8,822,334
Barley, bu	7,200,446	6,735,509	5,880,343
Rye, bu	2,183,260	2,170,853	1,526,542
Total grain, bu.	103,858,968	103,963,658	83,623,984
Flour to wheat, bu	14,264,325	13,287,520	9,942,140
Grand total, bu.	118,123,293	117,251,178	93,566,124

Exports of Breadstuffs from New York.

The following statement shows the foreign exports of flour and grain from New York for ten years:

	Flour, bbls.	Wheat, bush.	Corn, bush.
1870	1,950,234	18,446,035	487,792
1871	1,699,400	21,968,600	13,016,600
872	1,216,082	13,144,400	25,222,200
1873	1,655,331	27,801,800	15,587,500
1874	2,177,608	34,791,249	19,000,995
1875	1,954,'00	26,192,700	12,938,700
1876	1,987,304	24,135,233	16,077,082
1877	1,476,771	20,712,442	26,174,276
1878	2,557,709	55,062,873	26,580,871
1879	3,399,793	62,239,144	33,770,858

	Oats, bush.	Barley, bush.	Rye, bush.
1870	28,986	----	92,481
1871	47,308	98,700	525,800
1872	31,739	22,066	668,031
1873	49,700	19,400	1,069,100
1874	122,528	3,590	611,060
1875	138,800	1,500	206,980
1876	620,536	87,883	1,336,423
1877	250,063	2,302,022	2,051,563
1878	5,600,782	1,618,067	2,948,053
1879	502,224	156,902	3,558,240

Reducing flour to grain bushels, the totals compare as follows:

	Bushels.			Bushels.
1870	28,735,714	1875		49,249,100
1871	44,000,000	1876		52,293,652
1872	45,238,845	1877		58,871,221
1873	52,804,355	1878		104,740,191
1874	65,418,033	1879		117,226,312

Crop Returns.

The Agricultural Department at Washington publishes the following figures:

HARVEST.

	1878.	1879.
Wheat, bush	420,122,600	448,775,000
Corn, bush	1,383,218,750	1,544,899,000
Oats, bush	413,678,560	364,253,000
Rye, bush	23,842,790	23,640,500
Barley, bush	42,245,630	40,184,000
Buckwheat, bush	12,246,820	13,145,6 0
Cotton, bales	5,216,803	5,020,387
Tobacco, lbs	392,546,700	384,059,659
Hay, tons	39,908,096	35,648,600
Potatoes, bush	124,136,650	181,360,000

VALUE OF CROP.

	1878.	1879.
Wheat	$326,346,424	$499,008,000
Corn	441,153,405	580,259,000
Oats	101,945,830	120,853,000
Rye	13,502,826	15,555,000
Barley	24,483,315	23,655,300
Buckwheat	6,45 ,120	7,860,488
Cotton	190,851,611	231,000,000
Tobacco	22,137,428	24,454,501
Hay	285,543,752	325,851,280
Potatoes	73,059,125	78,971,000
Total value	$1,486,570,806	$1,904,490,659

CANAL COMMERCE.

IMPORTS.

STATEMENT of property left at Buffalo, on the Erie Canal, or which was left between that place and the Collector's Office next in order on the Canal; showing the quantity and average value of each article during the year 1879, going to the Western States, Canada and New York:

The Forest.

Articles. Product of Wood.	Quantity.	Reduced tons of 2,000 lbs.	Value of each article.
Boards and Scantling, feet	1,703,849	2,840	$23,854
Shingles, M	30	4	105
Timber, cubic feet	82,862	1,658	2,073
Wood, cords	253	708	1,012
Total		5,210	$27,043

Agriculture.

Product of Animals.

Hides, lbs	19,856	10	$3,376
Total		10	$3,376

Vegetable Food.

Wheat, bu	38,516	1,156	$43,908
Barley, bu	34,329	810	23,330
Oats, bu	200	3	70
Bran and ship stuffs, lbs	71,836	36	718
Peas and beans, bu	11,433	313	11,433
Apples, bbls	2,498	177	1,908
Total		2,525	$81,157

Manufactures.

Furniture, lbs	63,640	31	$6,364
Iron, pig, lbs	77,026,927	38,513	1,078,378
Bloom and bar iron, lbs	38,513	162	8,079
Castings and iron ware, lbs	717,169	354	43,036
Domestic salt, lbs	130,145,522	65,223	430,470
Foreign salt, lbs	1,273,608	637	9,'52
Total		104,920	$1,575,879

Merchandise.

Sugar, lbs	101,209,371	50,605	$8,602,797
Molasses, lbs	25,192,643	12,596	755,779
Nails, spikes and horse shoes, lbs	2,120,903	1,060	63,027
Iron and steel, lbs	11,308,043	5,654	339,241
Railroad iron, lbs	27,705,443	13,853	664,931
Flint, enamel, crockery and glassw., lbs	9,626,003	4,813	770,080
All oth. merchandise, lbs	142,270,775	71,134	7,114,539
Total		159,719	$18,310,994

Other Articles.

Stone, lime and clay, lbs	98,950,292	49,475	$395,801
Gypsum	1,246,100	626	1,246
Anthracite coal, lbs	188,297,574	94,131	282,402
Iron ore, lbs	16,322,722	8,161	47,336
Sundries, lbs	91,481,855	45,744	4,574,093
Total other articles		198,140	$5,300,878
Totals of all of the above articles		470,524	$25,299,027

FREE LIST.
Agriculture.
Product of Animals.

Lard, tallow and lard			
oil, lbs	16,472	8	$1,153
Cheese, lbs	66,492	33	3,990
Total		41	$5,143

Vegetable Food.

Flour, bbls	6,7 2	734	$40,752
Cornmeal, bbls	570	63	1,140
Dried Fruit, lbs	22,291,225		
Total		796	$41,892

All other Agricultural Products.

Cotton, lbs	33,410	17	$2,073
Unmanuf. tobacco, lbs	544,666	272	54,467
Hemp, lbs	1,148	1	72
Hops, lbs	30,000	15	3,000
Total		305	$60,212

Manufactures.

Domestic spirits, gals	3,765	15	$3,765
Leather, lbs	202,494	101	40,419
Bar and pig lead, lbs.	286,674	143	17,200
Domestic woolens, lbs	20,767,817	10.371	11,422,300
Domestic cottons, lbs.	30,335,374	15,168	6,067,074
Total		25,798	$17,550,758

Merchandise.

Coffee, lbs	3,977,021	1,989	$596,553
Totals of free list		28,920	$18,254,558

Grand total, tons			449,453
Grand total, value			$43,554,185

EXPORTS.

STATEMENT of property first cleared at the Collector's Office at Buffalo on the Erie Canal during the year 1879, showing the quantity, tolls and average value of each article, and also the whole amount of tolls received at that office on each article of property during the same period; also quantity, tons and tolls and average value on each article on the free list for 1879 coming from the Western States, Canada and New York:

The Forest.

Articles. Product of Wood.	Quantity.	Reduced to tons of 2,000 lbs.	Value of each article.
Boards and scantling, feet	107,158,316	178.597	$1,500,216
Shingles, M	34,690	4,325	131,104
Staves, lbs	56,029,617	28,015	392,207
Total of the forest, tons		210,937	
Total value			$2,023.524
Total tolls			54,037

Agriculture.
Product of Animals.

Hides, lbs	10,000	5	$1,700
Total prod't of animals, tons		5	
Total value			$1,700
Total tolls			

Vegetable Food.

Wheat, bu	29,708,699	891,260	$33,867,917
Rye, bu	1,445,401	40,471	910,602
Corn, bu	21,506,162	602,171	9,247,650
Barley, bu	299,757	7,193	209,830
Barley malt, bu	295,683	5,026	295,683
Oats, bu	908,373	14,533	317,931
Bran and ship stuff, lbs	318,460	159	3,185
Peas and beans, lbs	22,441	673	22,441
Total vegetable food, tons	1,561,486		
Total value			$44,875,239
Total tolls			529,177

Manufactures.

Furniture, lbs	8,500	4	$850
Pig iron, lbs	1,845,800	923	25,843
Bloom and bar iron, lbs	5,250	3	131
Castings and iron ware, lbs	900		54
Total manufactures, tons		930	
Total value			$26,876
Total tolls			244

Merchandise.

Sugar, lbs	41,100	21	$3,484
Nails,spikes and horse shoes, lbs	42,400	21	1.272
Iron and steel, lbs	40,000	23	1,290
Flint, enamel, crockery and glassw., lbs.	1,050	1	84
All oth. merchandise, lbs	1,160,836	580	58,042
Total merchandise, tons		643	
Total value			$64,092
Total tolls			46

Other Articles.

Stone, lime and clay, lbs	8,000	4	$32
Bituminous coal, lbs.	56,573,814	28,287	67,889
Petroleum or earth oil, crude and ref., bbls.	55,435	9,999	44,348
Sundries, lbs	7,924,043	3,962	396,204
Total other articles, tons		41,952	
Total value			$508,473
Total tolls			4,148

Totals of all of the above articles, tons	1,815,953		
Total value			$17,499,904
Total tolls			501,652

FREE LIST.
Boats.

Total miles boats cleared			2,684,414

The Forest.

Ashes, leached, bu	39,502	1,184	$1,185

Agriculture.
Product of Animals.

Pork, bbls	2,131	341	$25,562
Lard, tallow and lard, oil, bbls	35,500	18	2,485
Total		359	$28,047

Vegetable Food.

Flour, bbls	4,750	513	$28,500
Cornmeal, bbls	1,959	209	3,873
Total		722	$32,378

All other Agricultural Products.

Unmanuf. tobacco, lbs	2,500	1	$270
Clover and grass seed, lbs	108,240	54	4,042
Flax seed, lbs	22,233,587	11,119	500,368
Total		11,174	$504,660

Manufactures.

Domestic spirits, gals	46,950	187	$46,950
Leather, lbs	17,500	9	3,500
Oilmeal and cake, lbs.	729,549	365	14,591
Bar and pig lead, lbs.	179,493	90	10,770
Total		651	$75,811

Merchandise.

Coffee, lbs	300		$45
Totals of free list		14,090	$642,126

Grand total tons			1,830,843
Grand total value			$43,142,030
Grand total tolls			591,652

Imports and Exports.

IMPORTS.

	1877.	1878.	1879.
Lumber, ft	328,071	888,145	1,703,849
Timber, cubic ft	8,225	5,016	82,862
Shingles, M	177	10	30
Wood, cds	222	288	233
Cheese, lbs	....	56,189	66,492
Hides, lbs	459,117	28,055	19,856
Flour, bbls	8,107	4,319	6,792
Wheat, bu	4,711	16,000	38,516
Barley, bu	31,847	9.225	33,329
Clover and grass seed, lbs	30,230	....	....
Barley malt, bu	2,500	2,200	....
Oats, bu	2, 00	1,100	200
Bran, etc., lbs	188,769	87,500	71,836
Beans and peas, bu	2,453	1,221	11,433
Cornmeal, bbls	....	875	570
Live cattle, lbs	....	7,000	....
Flax seed, lbs	779,292	....	....
Hemp, lbs	53,301	513,506	1,448
Apples, bbls	7,045	20,772	2,498
Potatoes, bu	278	....	....
Dried fruit. lbs	6,605,652	8,583,803	22,2)1,225
Unmanufact'r'd tobacco, lbs	13,495	77,966	544,666
Dom. spirits, galls.	1,415	4,200	3,765
Fur and peltry, lbs	....	3,590	....
Lard, tallow and lard oil, lbs	....	49,890	16,472
Wool, lbs	....	9,126	....
Cotton, lbs	....	15,550	33,410
Hops, lbs	....	....	30,000
Dom. woolens, lbs.	4,485,588	8,681,641	20,767,817
Dom. cottons, lbs..	2,813,204	14,176,730	30,335,374
Furniture, lbs	....	290,015	63,649
Pig iron, lbs	10,667,195	21,749,199	77,026,917
Castings, etc., lbs	2,095,507	2,116,612	717,269
Bloom and bar iron, lbs	1,846,787	3,900,544	323,147
Bar and pig lead, lbs	....	9,023	286,674
Leather, lbs	80,925	82,383	202,094
Domestic salt, lbs..	125,558,812	153,039,875	130,445,522
Foreign salt, lbs	1,891,926	5,704,110	1,273,608
Sugar, lbs	5,063,817	65,467,013	101,209,371
Molasses, lbs	4,739,732	7,902,244	25,192,643
Coffee, lbs	233,403	813,566	3,977,021
Nails & spikes, lbs	1,432,820	1,972,561	2,120,903
Iron and steel, lbs	555,990	2,467,469	11,308,043
Railroad iron, lbs..	4,757,700	6,888,887	27,705,443
Crockery, etc., lbs.	209,680	5,670,704	9,626,003
All other mdse, lbs.	32,374,228	120,918,788	142 270,775
Stone, lime, etc., lbs	69,708,919	103,945,555	90,950,292
Gypsum, lbs	....	135,270	1,246,100
Anthracite coal, lbs.	419,219,210	216,324,286	184,267,574
Bitum's coal, lbs...	20,000,000	20,705,112	4,000,000
Sundries, lbs	60,011,365	78,261,703	91,181,855
Iron ore, lbs	6,580,090	4,686,700	16,322,722
Total tons of articles carried	395,080	415,846	499,453
Total value of articles carried	$12,310,455	$14,509,274	$43,554,185

EXPORTS.

	1877.	1878.	1879.
Lumber, ft	79,783,636	95,310,695	107,158,316
Staves, lbs	82,359,650	77,482,900	56,029,617
Shingles, M	30,542	29,283	34,000
Furs and peltry, lbs	100,689	....	....
Pork, bbls	36,007	15,198	2,131
Lard, tallow, etc., lbs	9,714.570	274,707	35,500
Hides, lbs	29,600	246,300	10,000
Timber, cubic feet.	....	700	....
Ashes, leached, bu.	....	7,000	30,502
Flour, bbls	4,216	2,811	4,750
Wheat, bu	13,270,120	25,833,877	29,708,699

	1877.	1878.	1879.
Rye, bu	977,334	1,823,736	1,445,401
Corn, bu	25,347,207	25,668,387	21,596,162
Barley, bu	1,078,368	900,562	299,757
Barley malt, bu	205,986	220,723	295,683
Oats, bu	3,407,280	4,327,117	908,373
Peas and beans, bu	514	27,215	22,441
Bran, etc., lbs	313.329	1,301,290	318,460
Apples, bbls	5,001	30	....
Potatoes, bu	114	977	....
Cornmeal, bbls	1.565	1,008	1,939
Dried fruit, lbs	2,809	....	....
Unmanufact'r'd tobacco, lbs	....	....	2,500
Clover and grass seed, lbs	4,403,475	1,064,907	108,240
Flax seed, lbs	2,628,271	....	22,238,547
Dom. spirits, galls.	52,495	74,040	46,950
Oilm'l and cake, lbs	2,644,806	931,427	729,549
Furniture, lbs	....	11.710	8,500
Pig iron, lbs	973,000	976,430	1,845,800
Bloom and bar iron, lbs	19,483	93,578	5,250
Castings, etc., lbs..	12,200	117,664	900
Bar and pig lead, lbs	2,055,748	81,411	179,493
Dom. cotton, lbs...	2,840	....	....
Domestic salt, lbs..	....	4,500	....
Sugar, lbs	9,000	19,500	41,100
Coffee, lbs	....	....	300
Crockery, lbs	32,960	21,510	1,050
Other mdse, lbs	541,878	828,205	1,160,836
Stone, lime, clay, lbs	3,224.015	1,980,305	8,000
Bitumin's coal, lbs.	58,409,941	79,640,631	56,579,814
Petroleum oil, cr'de and refined, bbls	....	155,371	55,435
Sundries	16,370,033	7,942,428	7,924,043
Nails & spikes, lbs.	....	66,800	42,400
Iron and steel, lbs.	....	7,000	40,000
Leather, lbs.	....	1,000	17,500
Total tons of articles carried	1,359,122	1,946,602	1,830,843
Total value of articles carried	$58,229,716	$43,466,806	$48,142,030
Tolls on boats on the canal	· 198	....	....
Total tolls	467,921 74	628,439 45	$591,652

FLOUR AND GRAIN RECAPITULATION.

The exports of flour and grain, compared for three years, are shown thus:

	1877. Canal opened May 8.	1878. April 16.	1879. May 8.
Flour, bbls	4,216	2,811	4,750
Wheat, bu	13,270,420	25.833,877	29,708,699
Corn, bu	25,347,207	25,668,387	21,596,192
Oats, bu	3,407,280	4,327,117	908,373
Barley, bu	1,078,368	900,562	299,757
Rye, bu	977,334	1,823,736	1.445,400
Total, bu	44,680,600	58,553,670	53,868,392
Flour to wheat, bu.	21,080	14,055	23,750
Grand total, bu	74,101,689	58,567,734	53,892,142

NOTE.—In 1874 there were shipped 104,754 bushels of barley malt, 153,853 bushels in 1875, 215,238 bushels in 1876, 205,986 bushels in 1877, 220,723 bushels in 1878 and 295,683 bushels in 1879. Of peas and beans 208 bushels in 1874, 3,844 bushels in 1875, 826 bushels in 1876, 544 bushels in 1877, 27,215 bushels in 1878 and 22,441 bushels in 1789.

Eastward and Westward Movement on Erie Canal.

The following statement shows the amount of freight by tons moved on the Erie Canal eastward and westward for ten years:

SHIPMENTS OF EASTWARD MOVING FREIGHT FROM BUFFALO.

Years.	Products of the forest, tons.	Products of animals, tons.	Veg'ble food, tons.
1870	402,390	250	802,541
1871	309,080	179	1,344,941
1872	347,695	52	1,322,981
1873	296,128	29	1,433,653
1874	216,893	38	1,164,392
1875	151,953	39	1,007,559
1876	121,379	23	783,122
1877	183,019	10,633	1,220,249
1878	231,433	2,686	1,635,082
1879	212,121	364	1,562,208

Years.	Other ag'l products, tons.	Manufactures, tons.	Merchandise, tons.
1870	610	5,152	767
1871	1,835	2,651	534
1872	1,411	564	367
1873	19	906	853
1874	204	846	530
1875	7	11,602	337
1876	29	373	335
1877	3,516	3,364	292
1878	532	1,406	472
1879	11,174	1,581	643

Years.	Other articles, tons.	Total tons.	Total value.
1870	93,194	1,393,904	$37,333,208
1871	112,944	1,742,157	99,426,629
1872	101,962	1,774,906	52,855,537
1873	94,035	1,825,623	49,772,070
1874	65,269	1,448,172	46,244,875
1875	38,051	1,219,538	40,608,163
1876	33,213	941,474	24,411,554
1877	38,049	1,459,122	38,229,716
1878	75,758	1,946,602	43,46 ,806
1879	41,952	1,830,843	$48,142,030

Total Amount of Tolls Received.

1870	$1,060,072 03	1875	$789,830 24
1871	1,389,909 81	1876	583,644 42
1872	1,416,049 31	1877	467,921 74
1873	1,415,634 33	1878	628,439 45
1874	1,196,780 55	1879	591,652 00

RECEIPTS OF EASTWARD MOVING FREIGHT AT BUFFALO.

Years.	Products of the forest, tons.	Products of animals, tons.	Veg'ble food, tons.
1870	4,276	11	9,266
1871	2,917	31	711
1872	3,467	187	2,337
1873	2,465	72	5,170
1874	2,014	37	15,174
1875	1,529	266	7,521
1876	1,507	88	3,152
1877	1,356	230	5,881
1878	1,874	72	7,211
1879	5,210	51	3,321

Years.	Other agr'l products, tons.	Manufactures, tons.	Merchandise, tons.
1870	....	78,066	103,967
1871	....	86,696	126,576
1872	....	101,519	151,560
1873	...	108,526	63,369
1874	3	99,305	36,145
1875	4	111,531	30,921
1876	....	69,547	4,627
1877	442	74,426	24,685
1878	304	204,893	106,060
1869	305	130,708	161,708

Years.	Other articles, tons.	Total tons.	Total value.
1870	438,333	633,819	$29,591,501
1871	321,662	538,593	23,124,220
1872	430,846	609,616	32,178,888
1873	522,051	701,653	19,568,226
1874	373,903	526,311	8,646,610
1875	403,465	555,237	9,193,785
1876	242,815	313,036	5,045,911
1877	287,760	395,080	12,310,455
1878	212,038	432,472	22,474,227
1879	198,140	499,453	$43,554,185

Canal Tolls.

The following table shows the aggregate receipts of tolls at Buffalo from the opening to the close of navigation for a series of years:

1879	$591,652 00	1874	$1,196,634 33
1878	628,439 45	1873	1,415,634 33
1877	467,921 74	1872	1,416,049 31
1876	583,644 42	1871	1,389,909 00
1875	789,830 24	1870	1,060,072 03

Canal opened May 8th, 1879; April 15th, 1878; May 8th, 1877; May 4th, 1876, and May 18th, 1875.

The tolls for 1879 from Buffalo to West Troy are as follows (distance 345 miles): Wheat, bushel of 60 lbs, 1c 0m 35f; corn, bushel of 56 lbs, 0c 9m 66f; rye, bushel of 56 lbs, 0c 9m 66f; barley, bushel of 48 lbs, 0c 8m 28f; oats, bushel of 32 lbs, 0c 5m 52f; malt, bushel of 34 lbs, 0c 5m 86f.

Canal Clearances.

The following statement shows the number of boats cleared from the opening to the closing of navigation for a series of years:

1879	8,708	1874	7,628
1878	9,047	1873	9,058
1877	6,938	1872	8,659
1876	4,853	1871	8,795
1875	6,349	1870	6,855

Canal Freights from Buffalo to New York.

The following table shows the ruling rates of freights to New York from Buffalo (tolls included, excepting for staves) on the dates specified in 1879:

1879.	Wheat, bu.	Corn, bu.	Oats, bu.	Pine lumber, M ft.	Staves, p. ton o'r toll.
May 8	5½c	5c	4c	$2 50	....
May 10	4½	4	3	2 50	....
May 17	4¾	4¼	3¼	2 50	....
May 21	4½	4	3	2 25	....
May 31	4½	4	3	2 30	$1 20
June 7	4	3⅝	2¾	2 25	1 20
June 14	4¼	3⅜	3	2 25	1 20
June 21	3¾	3¼	2½	2 25	1 00 @1 13
June 28	4½	4	3	2 25	1 00
July 5	5	4½	3½	2 40	1 13
July 12	5	4½	3¼	2 50	1 38
July 19	5	4⅝	3¾	2 60	1 44
July 26	5	5	3½	2 65	1 44
Aug. 2	6	5½	3⅝	2 75	1 50
Aug. 9	6	5½	3¾	2 90	1 63
Aug. 16	6¼	5⅜	4	3 00	1 75
Aug. 23	7½	6¾	4¾	3 50	1 88
Aug. 30	7¼	6½	4⅜	3 50	1 83
Sept. 6	7⅝	6½	4⅝	3 60	2 00
Sept. 13	7¾	7	4¾	3 60	2 00
Sept. 20	8½	7¾	5⅜	3 50	1 80
Sept. 27	9¼	8½	6	3 50	2 00
Oct. 4	7¼	7	4½	3 75	2 13
Oct. 11	7¼	6¼	4	4 00	2 25

1879.	Wheat, bu.	Corn, bu.	Oats, bu.	Pine Staves, Lumber, p. M. ft.	p. ton. o'er toll.
Oct. 18	9	8	5¾	3 85	2 00
Oct. 23, 24, 25	12	11	...	....	...
Oct. 25	11	9	7	4 00	2 38
Nov. 1	10	8	6	4 00	2 38
Nov. 8	10	9	6½	4 00	2 38
Nov. 15	10½	9	6¾	4 00	2 50
Nov. 22	10½	9½	6¾	4 00	2 50
Nov. 25	10½	...	...	....	....

Receipts at Tide-Water by Canal of Flour, Grain, Etc.

The following comparative table shows the quantity of the principal articles of produce left at tide-water from the commencement to the close of navigation in the years indicated:

Canal opened Flour, bbls	1877. May 8. 29,500	1878. April 15. 14,400	1879. May 8. 8,400
Wheat, bu	12,739,600	26,557,500	20,178,000
Corn, bu	23,623,100	25,304,600	30,074,000
Barley, bu	5,473,700	3,270,800	3,130,800
Rye, bu	1,282,700	2,149,300	2,053,900
Oats, bu	4,203,900	5,156,400	1,118,900
Malt, bu	607,500	500,000	379,400

Canal opened	1877. May 8.	1878. April 15.	1879. May 8.
Total grain, bu.	47,935,500	62,938,600	56,935,000
Flour to wheat, bu	147,500	72,000	42.000
Grand total, bu.	48,083,000	63,010,600	56,977,000

The receipts at tide-water by canal of the new crop of barley were 3,045,400 bushels, against 2,988,000 bushels in 1878, 5,120,500 bushels in 1877, 3,632,100 bushels in 1876, 3,833,600 bushels in 1875, 3,354,300 bushels in 1874, 2,130,800 bushels in 1873 and 4,147,100 bushels in 1872.

The receipts for ten years compare as follows (malt not included):

Year.	Flour, bbls.	Grain and flour, reduced, bush.
1870	452,700	37,641,205
1871	288,285	51,695,930
1872	137,300	51,986,660
1873	153,500	47,803,200
1874	165,200	48,687,200
1875	113,600	37,674,200
1876	37,100	30,845,300
1877	29,500	47,475,500
1878	14,400	62,510,600
1879	8,400	56,597,600

LIVE STOCK TRADE.

Range of Prices on the Principal Sales Day of Each Week During the Year.

We present below our usual tables showing the receipts and shipments of Live Stock by the different routes during the year 1879, with comparative tables of the total receipts, showing the growth of trade for the last 23 years, and a carefully prepared table of the range of prices on the principal market day of each week during the year:

RECEIPTS.

PER LAKE SHORE & MICHIGAN SOUTHERN RAILWAY.

Month.	Cattle cars.	Hogs cars.	Sheep cars.	Horses cars.
January	1,872	982	174	53
February	2,313	1,201	244	92
March	2,589	948	305	143
April	2,854	877	299	163
May	3,700	980	314	126
June	3,764	871	493	107
July	4,112	709	412	55
August	3,782	829	239	57
September	3,110	1,029	154	76
October	3,009	1,636	146	81
November	2,674	1,673	151	75
December	2,827	1,212	259	69

Month.	Cattle cars.	Hogs cars.	Sheep cars.	Horses cars.
Total, 1879	36,906	12,917	3, 90	1,097
1878	31,391	13,309	2,983	597
1877	24,485	7,744	2,144	610
1876	29,771	7,999	2,421	566
1875	22,935	7,300	2,131	915
1874	22,147	11,049	2,036	1,103
1873	22,401	14,078	2,362	1,687
1872	20,710	12,019	1,828	1,188
1871	17,080	7,252	1,655	722
1870	15,631	6,351	2,217	425

PER CANADA SOUTHERN RAILWAY.

Month.	Cattle cars.	Hogs cars.	Sheep cars.	Horses cars.
January	147	75	64	5
February	27	91	71	11
March	11	134	34	11
April	12	237	85	17
May	9	190	47	13
June	1	224	12	7
July	1	185	18	11
August	0	184	63	7
September	3	302	62	5
October	5	219	48	3
November	13	157	32	1
December	3	142	56	0
Total, 1879	232	2,141	592	91
1878	3,123	2,855	7,020	80
1877	4,174	1,006	649	50
1876	3,597	819	598	87
1875	3,477	837	562	81
1874	4,141	898	431	204

PER GRAND TRUNK RAILWAY.

Month.	Cattle cars.	Hogs cars.	Sheep cars.	Horses cars.
January	48	1	38	3
February	7	0	23	4
March	35	2	55	10
April	29	8	48	4
May	13	0	14	3
June	0	0	8	7
July	0	8	36	2
August	0	23	104	1
September	6	45	174	4
October	31	69	132	4
November	23	66	83	10
December	5	30	101	4
Total, 1879	202	252	816	56
1878	1,150	166	773	36
1877	278	67	227	39
1876	1,290	60	631	80
1875	2,004	76	879	37
1874	2,533	321	919	38

PER GREAT WESTERN RAILWAY.

Month.	Cattle cars.	Hogs cars.	Sheep cars.	Horses cars.
January	32	53	44	1
February	23	158	70	5
March	34	141	51	7
April	35	88	22	16
May	5	128	10	11
June	6	159	9	10
July	4	109	27	4
August	4	61	64	2
September	16	140	58	4
October	35	177	36	0
November	24	72	52	4
December	10	35	57	3
Total, 1879	228	1,321	500	67
1878	3,028	142	655	70
1877	2,409	485	496	67
1876	1,565	1,023	711	51
1875	1,192	1,065	633	98
1874	860	164	530	26

SHIPMENTS.

PER NEW YORK CENTRAL & HUDSON RIVER RAILWAY.

Month.	Cattle cars.	Hogs cars.	Sheep cars.	Horses cars.
January	1,694	708	224	60
February	2,114	963	285	84
March	2,194	797	319	149
April	2,485	790	322	156
May	3,302	864	276	124
June	3,167	758	422	101
July	3,447	629	415	47
August	3,208	717	830	49
September	2,650	973	266	67
October	2,503	1,370	214	69
November	2,259	1,359	212	68
December	2,399	895	286	53
Total, 1879	31,482	10,825	3,571	1,027
1878	26,763	10,924	3,120	634
1877	23,287	5,381	2,570	667
1876	26,325	5,571	2,320	366
1875	21,175	3,737	2,524	863
1874	24,288	9,207	2,234	1,207
1873	17,825	9,254	2,067	1,531
1872	18,045	6,642	2,117	354
1871	14,363	4,110	1,205	526
1870	13,022	26,78	1,399	313

PER NEW YORK, LAKE ERIE & WESTERN RAILWAY.

Month.	Cattle cars.	Hogs cars.	Sheep cars.	Horses cars.
January	219	117	86	6
February	198	254	115	13
March	379	275	117	24
April	368	257	68	33
May	275	310	37	31

Month.	Cattle cars.	Hogs cars.	Sheep cars.	Horses cars.
June	387	314	38	25
July	568	186	61	15
August	423	202	104	10
September	399	310	122	15
October	410	421	144	20
November	386	306	124	22
December	371	187	83	15
Total, 1879	4,403	3,133	1,089	233
1878	8,634	3,616	1,143	170
1877	8,385	2,206	949	104
1876	7,783	2,563	986	95
1875	4,252	2,366	1,058	106
1874	2,913	1,623	1,46	82
1873	4,050	3,339	1,408	171
1872	2,716	3,646	658	144
1871	6,945	2,666	702	153
1870	7,826	2,671	1,146	111

RECAPITULATION.

GRAND TOTAL RECEIPTS FOR 1879.

Routes.	Cattle cars.	Hogs cars.	Sheep cars.	Horses cars.
L. S. & M. S. R. R.	36,606	12,847	3,190	1,097
Canada Southern..	232	2,141	592	91
Grand Trunk	202	252	816	56
Great Western	228	1,321	500	67
Total, 1879	37,268	16,861	5,098	1,311
1878	38,625	17,947	5,161	850
1877	31,348	10,598	3,813	766
1876	3,223	10,001	4,319	784
1875	30,203	9,281	4,205	1,137
1874	29,682	12,141	3,919	1,371

GRAND TOTAL SHIPMENTS FOR 1879.

Routes.	Cattle cars.	Hogs cars.	Sheep cars.
N. Y. C. & H. R. R. R...	31,482	10,825	3,571
Erie Railway	4,403	3,133	1,089
Total, 1879	35,885	13,958	4,660

GROWTH OF THE TRADE.

The following table shows the growth of the trade since 1857:

Year	Cattle head.	Hogs head.	Sheep head.	Horses head.
1857	108,263	117,108	307,519	
1858	134,073	92,194	315,731	
1859	103,337	73,619	189,579	
1860	156,972	85,770	145,354	
1861	141,679	101,679	238,952	
1862	129,433	103,671	524,976	
1863	151,789	92,128	474,849	
1864	135,797	301,629	155,959	
1865	212,839	300,014	207,208	
1866	275,091	552,831	341,560	
1867	257,872	697,440	239,913	
1868	265,105	470,578	385,815	7,773
1869	347,871	794,272	381,450	12,038
1870	386,057	730,519	561,447	7,896
1871	384,294	886,014	551,131	13,319
1872	379,086	1,145,109	606,748	20,786
1873	409,738	1,662,500	733,400	23,386
1874	504,594	1,431,800	783,800	21,036
1875	513,530	1,067,300	841,100	18,187
1876	615,790	1,150,210	871,928	12,542
1877	569,915	1,128,770	763,600	12,557
1878	657,809	2,063,765	1,032,225	13,602
1879	633,556	1,916,015	1,019,600	20,976

STOCK SLAUGHTERED.

The estimated amount of stock slaughtered in this city for the last six years is as follows:

Year	Cattle head.	Hogs head.	Sheep head.
1874	35,073	173,300	96,800
1875	19,656	159,500	118,200
1876	25,651	208,560	103,678
1877	29,158	17,000	47,500
1878	53,125	387,210	175,265
1879	23,511	310,845	87,600

24

RANGE OF PRICES.

The following exhibit shows the prevailing prices per cwt. during the principal market day in each week on cattle, hogs, sheep and lambs:

Cattle.

	Common to fair.	Good to best.	Stockers & feeders.
January			
4....	$2 00@3 75	$4 10@5 50	$2 00@3 25
11....	2 00 3 75	4 0@5 50	2 00 a 3 00
18....	2 25@3 85	4 30@5 87	2 75@3 25
25....	2 15@3 90	4 00@4 50	2 75@3 25
February			
2....	2 00@3 90	4 00@5 23	2 90@3 50
8....	2 00@4 15	4 25 - 5 25	2 90 a 3 50
15....	2 00@4 35	4 45@5 50	3 00 3 50
22....	2 15 @ 4 35	4 40@5 30	3 25@3 05
March			
1 ...	2 00@4 35	4 40 a 5 30	3 50 a 4 00
8 ...	2 10 4 15	4 25 5 10	3 25@4 00
15....	2 00@4 15	4 25@5 15	3 25@3 85
22....	2 25@4 40	4 50@5 80	3 00 a 3 75
29....	2 50@4 50	4 60@5 32	3 00 a 3 75
April			
5....	3 00@4 65	4 70@5 50	2 75@3 75
12....	3 00@4 40	4 50 a 5 60	3 50@3 85
19....	2 50 - 4 25	4 30@5 40	3 40 a 3 85
26....	2 50 a 4 25	4 30@5 62	3 40@3 85
May			
3....	3 00@4 60	4 40@5 50	3 30@3 85
10....	3 00 a 4 30	4 40@5 25	3 30 a 4 25
17....	3 00@4 60	4 70 a 5 70	3 75@4 25
24....	3 00@4 50	4 60@5 60	3 30 a 4 25
31....	3 00@4 40	4 50@5 40	3 50@4 40
June			
8...	2 50@4 25	4 40 a 5 25	3 00@4 00
15...	2 75@4 25	4 30 a 5 25	3 00@4 17
21...	2 50@4 35	4 40@5 00	2 90@4 15
28...	2 50@4 50	4 50 a 5 25	2 75 a 3 75
July			
5....	2 50@4 25	4 35@5 00	2 65@3 50
12...	2 25@4 25	4 35@5 00	2 75@3 50
19...	2 50@4 25	4 35@5 40	2 25 a 3 35
26...	2 00 a 4 10	4 20 a 5 12	2 75 a 3 35
August			
3...	1 75@4 10	4 20@5 25	2 75@3 25
9...	1 75 a 4 15	4 25@5 25	2 75@3 25
16...	2 00@4 25	4 35@5 35	2 75@3 25
23...	2 25@4 40	4 50@5 40	2 75 a 3 25
30...	2 25@4 40	4 50 5 25	2 75@3 40
September			
6...	2 25@4 40	4 50@5 35	2 90@3 40
13...	2 00 a 4 40	4 50 a 5 50	2 50 a 3 40
20...	1 50@4 00	4 20@5 15	2 40@3 40
27...	2 00@3 90	4 10@5 10	2 50@3 50
October			
4....	2 00@4 00	4 10@5 35	2 25@3 40
11...	2 00@4 00	4 10@5 35	2 25@3 40
18...	2 00@4 10	4 15@5 10	2 25@3 45
25...	2 00@4 35	4 40 a 5 25	2 50@3 40
November			
1...	2 00@4 25	4 30@5 25	2 40@3 40
8...	1 80@3 90	4 00@5 12	2 40@3 10
15...	2 00@3 90	4 00@5 00	2 35@3 00
22...	2 15@4 15	4 30@5 75	2 20@3 10
29...	2 00 a 4 15	4 30@5 35	2 40@3 10
December			
6...	2 25@4 25	4 30@5 00	2 40@3 10
13...	2 50@4 50	4 60@5 50	2 50@3 40
20...	2 15@4 50	4 55@6 75	2 45@3 35
27...	1 75@4 25	4 30@5 05	2 40@3 15

Hogs.

	Yorkers.	Medium and heavy.
January		
4........	$2 65 - 2 90	$2 25@3 10
11........	2 95@3 10	2 25 a 3 25
18........	2 90@3 20	2 25@3 45
25........	3 20@3 60	2 75@3 75
February		
2........	3 50@3 85	2 50@4 05
8........	3 75@4 10	3 00@4 33
15........	3 90@4 13	2 75@4 35
22........	4 10@4 20	3 75@4 30
March		
1........	3 90@4 35	3 75@4 40
8........	3 90@4 15	3 75@4 35
15........	3 75@4 07	3 50@4 15
22........	3 90@4 50	3 50@4 25
29........	3 90@4 50	3 25@4 60
April		
5........	3 75@4 00	3 25@4 25
12........	3 80@4 00	3 65@4 35
19........	3 60@3 80	3 50@4 25
26........	3 50@3 70	2 75@4 00
May		
3........	3 60@3 70	2 75@3 80
10........	3 60@3 80	2 75@3 90
17........	3 70@3 80	3 50@3 85
24........	3 60@3 75	3 25@3 77
31........	3 50@3 70	3 25@3 75

Hogs (continued).

	Yorkers.	Medium and heavy.
June		
8............	3 60 a 3 70	3 25@3 70
15............	3 25@4 07	3 25@4 15
21............	3 90 a 4 10	3 25@4 15
28............	3 90@4 05	3 20@4 05
July		
5............	3 90@4 05	3 25@4 10
12............	4 10@4 15	3 25@4 17
19............	3 65@3 90	3 25@4 00
26............	3 75@4 00	3 25@4 00
August		
3............	3 70@3 80	3 00@3 75
9............	3 15@3 85	3 00@3 90
16............	3 50@4 30	3 25@4 10
23............	3 50@3 80	3 00@3 75
30............	3 40@3 60	3 00@3 63
September		
6............	3 50@3 75	3 00@3 70
13............	3 40@3 80	3 00@3 90
20............	3 50@4 05	3 10@4 00
27............	3 50@3 85	3 20@4 00
October		
4............	3 50@3 90	2 75@3 80
11............	3 70@4 20	2 25@4 15
18............	3 75@4 05	3 00@4 07
25............	3 60@3 95	2 75@4 00
November		
1............	3 60@4 10	3 00@4 10
8............	3 40@3 70	2 50@3 90
15............	3 45@3 95	3 15@4 00
22............	4 00@4 30	3 25@4 35
29............	3 85@4 00	3 40@4 30
December		
6............	4 25@4 60	3 55@4 90
13............	4 25@4 60	3 65@4 90
20............	4 15@4 25	3 75@4 75
27............	4 50@5 00	3 75@5 00

Sheep and Lambs.

	Western sheep.	Canada lambs.
January		
4...	$3 25@4 50	$1 25@5 37
11...	3 60@5 00	4 75@5 00
18...	3 25@4 40	4 75@4 90
25...	3 75@5 00	4 75@5 00
February		
2...	4 00@5 25	5 25@5 50
8...	4 10@5 50	5 00@5 75
15...	4 25@5 75	5 00@5 75
22...	4 25@5 30	5 00@5 75
March		
1...	4 25@5 25	5 10@5 75
8...	4 25@5 75	5 00@5 75
15...	4 40@5 70	5 00@5 75
22...	4 25@5 60	5 00@5 50
29...	4 50@6 00	5 00@5 50
April		
5...	4 90@6 25	No sales
12...	4 95@6 25	"
19...	4 75@6 12	"
26...	3 75@6 00	"
May		
3...	3 75@6 00	"
10...	3 90@5 80	"
17...	4 00@5 25	"
24...	3 25@5 25	"
31...	3 25@5 25	"
June		
8...	3 25@5 25	"
15...	3 25@5 75	"
21...	3 25@5 50	"
28...	2 40@5 00	"
July		
5...	3 00@5 00	"
12...	3 20@5 00	
19...	3 50@4 75	5 40@5 80
26...	3 00@4 75	5 40@5 80
August		
3...	3 00@4 75	4 75@5 40
9...	3 00@4 75	5 25@5 50
16...	3 00@5 80	5 00@5 35
23...	3 00@4 75	5 00@5 35
30...	3 00@4 70	5 00@5 25
September		
6...	3 00@4 70	4 50@5 00
13...	3 00 a 4 75	4 50@4 75
20...	2 90@4 50	4 50@4 75
27...	3 00@4 50	4 50@4 75
October		
4...	3 00@4 35	4 25@4 60
11...	3 00@4 50	4 40@4 75
18...	3 00@4 50	4 85@5 20
25...	3 25@4 25	5 00@5 40
November		
1...	3 25@4 25	5 0 @5 20
8...	3 25@4 50	4 60@5 00
15...	3 15@4 25	4 50@4 70
22...	3 00@4 50	5 00@5 25
29...	3 25@4 50	4 25@5 20
December		
6...	3 25 - 4 50	5 15@5 37
13...	3 75@4 50	5 75@6 00
20...	3 50 5 50	5 75@6 25
27...	3 75@5 75	6 25@6 50

WILLIAM THURSTONE,

COMPILER AND PUBLISHER OF

COMMERCIAL REPORTS, STATISTICS, &c.

BUFFALO, N. Y.

EXPERT OF THE BUREAU OF STATISTICS.

THE WESTERN ELEVATING COMPANY

OF BUFFALO.

WILLIAM H. ABELL, ...President.
D. S. AUSTIN, ... Vice President.
P. G. COOK, Jr.,........ .. ..Secretary and Treasurer.

Office, No. 12 Commercial Block, corner Main and Ohio Streets, Buffalo, N. Y.

☞ This Company controls 32 Elevators and Transfers; and the quantity of Grain handled in 1879 was 74,405,626 bushels.

FREE TRADE FLOATING ELEVATOR CO.

No. 17 CENTRAL WHARF (up stairs), BUFFALO.

"FREE TRADE" ELEVATOR, "FREE CANAL" ELEVATOR.

Capacity for Transfering Grain, 100,000 bushels each for each 24 hours.

CHARLES J. MANN, Manager.

LOUIS PFOHL.   JOHN KENNEDY.

PFOHL & KENNEDY,

COMMISSION MERCHANTS

AND DEALERS IN

WET FLOUR AND GRAIN.

Office, No. 36 Main Street, BUFFALO.

WHITNEY & GIBSON,

COMMISSION MERCHANTS

No. 14 CENTRAL WHARF,

BUFFALO, N. Y.

M. L. CRITTENDEN,

COMMISSION AND SHIPPING MERCHANT

No. 28 CENTRAL WHARF,

BUFFALO, N. Y.

WILLIAM PETRIE.   G. R. GREEN.   W. F. CHANDLER.

WM. PETRIE & CO.

FORWARDING AND COMMISSION MERCHANTS

11 CENTRAL WHARF,

SECOND FLOOR.   BUFFALO, N. Y.

S. S. BROWN,

GRAIN FORWARDING and COMMISSION MERCHANT

No. 20 CENTRAL WHARF,

BUFFALO, N. Y.

WILLIAM H. VOSBURGH.   HOWARD H. BAKER.

VOSBURGH & BAKER,

SHIP CHANDLERS, GROCERS AND SAILMAKERS

WILLIAMS' BLOCK,   BUFFALO, N. Y.

NATHANIEL ROCHESTER,

SHIPPING AND COMMISSION MERCHANT

GRAIN AND PROVISIONS.

No. 20 Central Wharf,   BUFFALO, N. Y.

REFERENCES.—FIRST NATIONAL BANK, THIRD NATIONAL BANK, BANK OF BUFFALO.

CHARLES A. SWEET,

MANUFACTURER OF AND DEALER IN

MICHIGAN AND CANADA RIVED HOOPS

ROUND SHAVED HOOPS,

Also, Flour, Fruit and Sugar Barrel Staves and Heading, and Cooperage generally.

No. 14 Central Wharf (Up Stairs),   BUFFALO, N. Y.

THORNTON VAN VLIET,

GRAIN, FORWARDING & COMMISSION MERCHANT

No. 20 CENTRAL WHARF,

BUFFALO, N. Y.

W. MEADOWS,

GRAIN COMMISSION

BUFFALO, N. Y.

A. L. LOTHRIDGE.   E. GALLAGHER.   J. COLLINS.

LOTHRIDGE, GALLAGHER & CO.

COMMISSION and FORWARDING MERCHANTS

Agents for the Baxter Steam Canal Boat Transportation Co.

2d Floor, 10 Central Wharf,   **BUFFALO, N. Y.**

Grain, Lumber, Coal, Iron, Stone, Oil and other heavy freights forwarded from Lake Ports to Troy, Albany, New York, Philadelphia, Baltimore and intermediate points, and through rates given if desired.

AGENTS AND CONSIGNEES:

M. F. JAMES, 105 Broad Street, New York.   *JEFF COLLINS, West Troy and Albany.*
DAVID FALES & CO., 14 South Street, New York.   *THORN & POMEROY, Utica, N. Y.*

F. W. FISKE.   A. M. HAZARD.

F. W. FISKE & CO.

COMMISSION MERCHANTS

No. 29 CENTRAL WHARF,

BUFFALO, N. Y.

E. W. EAMES,

COMMISSION MERCHANT

CENTRAL WHARF, BUFFALO, N. Y.

ALFRED P. WRIGHT.   ALBERT J. WRIGHT.

A. P. WRIGHT & SON,

COMMISSION MERCHANTS

BUFFALO, N. Y.

BISSELL, FINN & CO.

FORWARDING and COMMISSION MERCHANTS

14 CENTRAL WHARF, BUFFALO, N. Y.

CANAL TRANSPORTATION A SPECIALTY.

J. F. SCHOELLKOPF.   GEO. H. MATHEWS.

SCHOELLKOPF & MATHEWS,

PROPRIETORS OF

NIAGARA FALLS AND FRONTIER MILLS

CAPACITY, 1000 BARRELS PER DAY.

MILLERS OF PATENT

MINNESOTA WHEAT FLOUR.

Office, 20 Central Wharf, BUFFALO, N. Y.

CYRUS CLARKE.   C. CLARKE VAN DEVENTER.

CYRUS CLARKE & CO.

Produce Commission Merchants

14 MAIN STREET,

BUFFALO, N. Y.

KINNE, WILBER & CO.

COMMISSION AND SHIPPING MERCHANTS

BUFFALO, N. Y.

RED JACKET DISTILLERY.
ESTABLISHED 1848.

THOMAS CLARK,
MANUFACTURER OF

EXTRA FINE OLD WHISKIES

ALCOHOL AND COLOGNE SPIRITS.

Cor. Washington and Perry Sts.,   BUFFALO, N. Y.

C. H. ARTHUR & CO.

GRAIN DEALERS

Shipping and Commission Merchants.

No. 31 Central Wharf,   BUFFALO, N. Y.

R. R. HEFFORD,
FORWARDER AND DEALER IN

ANTHRACITE,   **COALS.**   BITUMINOUS,
CANNEL,   BLOSSBURG.

Office, No. 2 Main St. and No. 1 Central Wharf.   Docks, opposite foot of Main St.

BUFFALO, N. Y.

Railroad Iron, Iron Ore, and other Heavy Freight Docked and Forwarded.

JOHN B. GRIFFIN, President.   CHAS. C. McDONALD, Sec'y and Treas'r.

INCORPORATED 1880.

THE QUEEN CITY MILLING CO.

Office, 6 Central Wharf and 12 Main St., (2d floor), BUFFALO, N. Y.

MANUFACTURE

Queen City Milling Co.'s Best Patent; J. B. Griffin & Co.'s Patent, Family and Bakers; Queen City Mills (Straight), Barrels and (200 lbs.) Export Sacks; Erie Mills Bakers,' Favorite Minnesota; also, Clear, Rye and Foundry Flour, Mill Feed, &c.

JEWETT M. RICHMOND.   M. M. RICHMOND.   ALONZO RICHMOND.

J. M. RICHMOND & CO.

STORAGE, ELEVATING,

COMMISSION AND FORWARDING MERCHANTS

16 Central Wharf, BUFFALO, N. Y.

GRAIN CLEANING AND DRYING.

BRUNDIGE, BRUCE & CO.

COMMISSION AND SHIPPING MERCHANTS

5 CENTRAL WHARF, BUFFALO, N. Y.

WILLIS C. JACUS.   JOSEPH E. HADCOCK.

W. C. JACUS & CO.

FORWARDING AND COMMISSION

15 CENTRAL WHARF, BUFFALO, N. Y.

C. F. STERNBERG,

COMMISSION MERCHANT

No. 3 Central Wharf, BUFFALO, N. Y.

Sternberg Elevators connecting with New York Central Railroad.

NATIONAL MILLS

Nos. 212 TO 220 ERIE STREET.

MANUFACTURERS OF

"THORNTON & CHESTER'S BEST," "PATENT," "GLOBE," "WHITE LILY," "FRANKLIN," AND GRAHAM FLOUR.

CORN MEAL AND FEED OF ALL KINDS

THORNTON & CHESTER.

A. S. CARPENTER.   WM. AVERY.   JAS. L. BREED.

PEOPLE'S LINE.

CARPENTER, AVERY & CO.

FORWARDING and COMMISSION MERCHANTS

No. 13 CENTRAL WHARF.

UP STAIRS.   BUFFALO, N. Y.

SHERMAN BROS.

FORWARDING AND COMMISSION

No. 92 Lloyd Street, BUFFALO, N. Y.

CEMENT, PLASTER, SALT, LIME, GRAIN, &c.

HERMAN J. HALL & CO.

GRAIN DEALERS

AND COMMISSION MERCHANTS.

26 Central Wharf, BUFFALO, N. Y.

FRED. H. GATCHELL. J. F. HAGER, JR.

GATCHELL & HAGER,

FORWARDING AND COMMISSION MERCHANTS

No. 12 CENTRAL WHARF,

BUFFALO, N. Y.

ESSER, OGDEN & CO.

NORTH BUFFALO MILLS

E. O. & Co.'s "Best," "Banner," "Stella," "Buffalo."

OFFICE, COIT BLOCK, No. 20 WEST SWAN ST.

BUFFALO, N. Y.

J. T. CRAWFORD,

AGENT FOR

The Syracuse Fine Salt Company,
The Onondaga Coarse Salt Association,
The American Dairy Salt Company (Limited).

No. 30 CENTRAL WHARF,

BUFFALO, N. Y.

E. J. NEWMAN & CO.

MANUFACTURERS OF

AKRON CEMENT

MANUFACTURERS OF

AKRON FALLS FLOUR.

CITY AGENTS FOR

NIAGARA FALLS FLOUR.

Works at Akron, N. Y.   *50 River St., BUFFALO, N. Y.*

E. N. COOK & CO.

DISTILLERS

Office and Free Warehouses, 32 and 34 Main Street.

Distillery and Bonded Warehouses, 479, 481, 483, 485, 487, 489 and 491 Spring St.

BUFFALO, N. Y.

WITTER & SERGEANT,

FORWARDING AND COMMISSION

MERCHANTS,

No. 32 CENTRAL WHARF, Up Stairs.

WM. E. WITTER.   **BUFFALO, N. Y.**   A. J. SERGEANT.

HARVEY & HENRY,

BUFFALO CITY FLOUR MILLS

MANUFACTURERS OF

HIGH GRADES OF FLOUR.

BUFFALO, N. Y.

GEORGE SANDROCK,

PRODUCE COMMISSION MERCHANT

28 CENTRAL WHARF, BUFFALO, N. Y.

REFERENCE.—BANK OF COMMERCE, BUFFALO.

CANADIAN BARLEY A SPECIALTY.

EMPIRE LINE.

SHAVER, BETTS & HOMER,

FORWARDING AND COMMISSION MERCHANTS

No. 9 Central Wharf, BUFFALO, N. Y.

JACOB SHAVER, JR. IRA BETTS. ADAM HOMER.

FRANK WILLIAMS & CO.

DEALERS IN AND SHIPPERS OF

COAL.

No. 4 Central Wharf, BUFFALO, N. Y.

GAS, STEAM AND DOMESTIC COALS AT WHOLESALE AND RETAIL.

The best facilities for receiving and forwarding COAL on consignment.

Yard cor. Carroll and Alabama Sts., Docks on Blackwell Canal, opp. Watson Elevator.

J. C. ANTHONY. E. L. ANTHONY.

J. C. ANTHONY & SON,

FORWARDING and PRODUCE COMMISSION

No. 21 Central Wharf, BUFFALO, N. Y.

AGENTS FOR BUFFALO, NEW YORK & ITHACA LINE.

Receivers and Shippers of Grain, Lumber, Shingles, Staves, and all kinds of Coarse Freight to all points along the Erie and Lateral Canals.

☞ DOCKS AT ERIE BASIN.

J. A. CAMPBELL.   S. M. RATCLIFFE.

J. A. CAMPBELL & CO.

GRAIN AND COMMISSION MERCHANTS

No. 33 Central Wharf, BUFFALO, N. Y.

J. S. HEATH.   WM. MORSE.   A. NELSON.

HEATH, MORSE & CO.

FORWARDING AND COMMISSION

MERCHANTS.

Office, 11 Central Wharf, BUFFALO, N. Y.

LLOYD STREET MILL.

MEECH & CO.

MILLERS AND DEALERS IN

FLOUR, OATS, CORN

MEAL AND MILL FEED.

Nos. 32, 34 and 36 Lloyd Street,   BUFFALO, N. Y.

M. N. JONES.   H. R. JONES.

MILES JONES' SONS,

WHOLESALE PROVISION DEALERS,

PORK PACKERS AND HAM CURERS

ALL KINDS LAKE FISH.

Cor. PRIME and DAYTON STREETS, BUFFALO, N. Y.

E. B. COLLINS,

COMMISSION MERCHANT

No. 25 CENTRAL WHARF (UP STAIRS).

BUFFALO, N. Y.

ESTABLISHED 1860.

H. MORSE & CO.

FORWARDING AND COMMISSION MERCHANTS

16 CENTRAL WHARF,

BUFFALO, N. Y.

HENRY C. ROBE'S LINE.

Grain, Flour, Lumber, Coal, Iron, Oil and other Heavy Freights transported from Lake Ports to Troy, Albany, New York, Philadelphia, Baltimore and intermediate Points, and through Bill of Lading given.

OFFICE, 18 CENTRAL WHARF,   BUFFALO, N. Y.

AGENTS AND CONSIGNEES:

H. W. MARKS, 18 Central Wharf,   E. B. BROOKE & CO., 7 South Street, New York.
Buffalo, N. Y.   C. H. GAGE & CO., 105 Broad Street, New York.
COLLINS & POTTER, West Troy, N. Y.

E. B. BROOKE.   P. M. LAWRENCE.

E. B. BROOKE & CO.

FORWARDING AGENTS AND CONSIGNEES

FOR FREIGHT ON ERIE CANAL FROM THE WEST.

OFFICE, 7 SOUTH STREET,   NEW YORK.

WM. E. HINGSTON,

FOREIGN COMMISSION MERCHANT

Central Wharf, BUFFALO, N. Y.

Special Attention given to the introduction of American Products in the European Markets.

AGENT FOR JAMES & HAGEMANN, HAVRE, FRANCE.

THOS. M. RYAN,

FORWARDER AND

COMMISSION MERCHANT

No. 24 CENTRAL WHARF, BUFFALO, N. Y.

Grain and Coarse Freights contracted to and from all points East and West.

SCHAEFER & BRO.

IMPORTERS IN

CANADA BARLEY

WHOLESALE DEALERS IN

NEW YORK STATE AND WESTERN BARLEY.

AND MALTSTERS.

No. 42 and 44 LLOYD STREET,   .   BUFFALO, N. Y.

J. L. RING.   HENRY BRINKMANN.

J. L. RING & CO.

BUFFALO FARINA MILLS

No. 30 WILKESON STREET, Cor. FOURTH.

CHOICE FAMILY AND HAXALL FLOUR.

Farina, Pearl Barley, Split Peas, Corn Meal and Oatmeal, &c.

DEALERS IN CORN AND OATS AND ALL KINDS OF FEED.

Market Mills, 20 WEST MARKET ST.   RING & BRINKMANN, Prop's.

TRADE MARK.

CORNELL LEAD CO.

MANUFACTURERS OF

WHITE LEAD

LEAD PIPE, SHEET and BAR LEAD.

OFFICE AND WORKS:

Cor. Delaware and Virginia Streets.

A. P. THOMPSON, Pres. HENRY SPAYTH, Treas.
S. DOUGLAS CORNELL, Vice-Pres. SHELDON THOMPSON, Sec'y

Forfeited If Adulterated.

PRATT & CO.

TERRACE SQUARE, BUFFALO.

IRON, NAILS, SPIKES

BOLTS, NUTS and WASHERS.

HARDWARE OF EVERY DESCRIPTION

For BUILDERS, MANUFACTURERS and MECHANICS.

RAILROAD SUPPLIES

Metals and Tools of All Kinds. Dock, Vessel and Pier Iron Work,
Chains, Rope, Belting, Etc.

CUTLERY, SILVER PLATED WARE

And General Household and Boat Supplies.

WHOLESALE AND RETAIL.

"THE AMERICAN BLOCK."

ADAM, MELDRUM & ANDERSON,

IMPORTERS, JOBBERS AND RETAILERS OF

DRY GOODS, CARPETS & UPHOLSTERY GOODS

*396, 398, 400 and 402 Main Street, through to and including 209, 211,
213 and 215 Pearl Street,*

BUFFALO, N. Y.

GEO. W. TIFFT, SONS & CO.

ENGINES, BOILERS AND MACHINERY

ARCHITECTURAL CASTINGS,

PROPELLER WHEELS AND MACHINERY GENERALLY

BUFFALO, N. Y.

BUFFALO INSURANCE CO.

CAPITAL, $200.000,

Invested in Government Registered Bonds.

FIRE, LAKE AND CANAL RISKS

WRITTEN AT CURRENT RATES.

OFFICE, 44 AND 46 MAIN STREET.

PASCAL P. PRATT, President.   JAMES D. SAWYER, Vice-Pres.   EDWARD B. SMITH, Secretary.

NATHANIEL HALL,

FIRE, LIFE AND ACCIDENT INSURANCE

No. 3 MAIN STREET, CORNER OHIO,

BUFFALO, N. Y.

REPRESENTS THE LARGEST LINE OF LEADING INSURANCE COMPANIES OF ANY AGENCY IN BUFFALO.

HOWARD IRON WORKS, BUFFALO, N. Y.

MANUFACTURERS OF

MACHINERY FOR GRAIN ELEVATORS

THEY HAVE FURNISHED THE MACHINERY FOR

MUNGER, WHEELER & CO. AIR LINE ELEVATOR..........CHICAGO, ILLS.
VINCENT, NELSON & CO. ELEVATOR...................... "   "
ARMOUR, DOLE & CO. C ELEVATOR .... "   "
ARMOUR, DOLE & CO. D ELEVATOR .... "   "
MUNGER, WHEELER & CO. IOWA ELEVATOR............... "   "
MUNGER, WHEELER & CO. ST. PAUL ELEVATOR........... "   "
N. Y., LAKE ERIE & WESTERN R'Y CO. ELEVATOR........BUFFALO, N. Y.
COMMERCIAL ELEVATOR .... "   "
WHEELER ELEVATOR .... "   "
SILO ELEVATOR, HAMBURG, GERMANY, and others.

THE UNION DRY DOCK CO.

SHIP YARD AND DRY DOCKS

On Buffalo Creek. foot of Chicago St., Opp. Niagara Elevator, BUFFALO, N. Y.

Ship Building, Repairing, and every description of Carpenter, Caulking, Joiner, Blacksmith and Spar Work done to order. TWO LARGE DRY DOCKS.

We are prepared to do all kinds of repairing on the shortest possible notice, and in the most thorough manner. Our Dry Docks have a LARGE DERRICK, for hoisting Wheels, Rudders, or heavy work from the Creek into the Docks, which saves the expense of landing.

On hand and for sale all kinds of SHIP TIMBER, PLANK, KNEES, ASH and PINE SPARS, &c.

Particular attention paid to Spar work, by an experienced SPAR MAKER.

M. M. DRAKE, Superintendent.

H. J. SHUTTLEWORTH,

BANKER and BROKER in

STOCKS, GRAIN AND PETROLEUM

No. 10 EAST SENECA ST., BUFFALO, N. Y.

Strictly Commission. Special facilities for carrying on margin.

HALL & SONS,

MANUFACTURERS OF

FIRE BRICK

AND DEALERS IN

FIRE CLAY, FIRE SAND, FIRE MORTAR, &c.,

AND

ARCHITECTURAL + TERRA + COTTA

From the Celebrated Perth Amboy Terra Cotta Company.

SOLE AGENTS

For the State of New York for

MOORE'S CHAMPION BOILER FEEDER

THE ONLY SURE

PREVENTATIVE OF SCALE ON STEAM BOILERS

Office, 15 Clinton St., BUFFALO, N. Y.

WITHOUT THE USE OF COMPOUNDS.

ANK**

Accounts of merchants, manufacturers and business men generally, respectfully solicited. **COLLECTIONS PROMPTLY MADE** at most favorable rates, according to the extent of the business furnished.

Approved Commercial Paper discounted at the uniform rate of

7 PER CENT. PER ANNUM,

To depositors keeping otherwise satisfactory accounts with this bank.

Especial attention given to the business of Dealers in and Consignees of Grain, Western Produce and Live Stock of all kinds.

We beg leave also to announce having opened a direct account with the well-known Bankers,

Messrs. BROWN, SHIPLEY & CO., of London, England.

WE ARE PREPARED TO DRAW

STERLING BILLS, AVAILABLE IN ANY PART OF THE WORLD

AT LOWEST CURRENT PRICES, AVOIDING ALL AGENTS' COMMISSIONS.

FOREIGN EXCHANGE BOUGHT AT NEW YORK MARKET RATES.

CHARLES T. COIT, *President.* R. PORTER LEE, *Cashier.*

ESTABLISHED 1854.

SCHOOL and CHURCH FURNITURE

SETTEES A SPECIALTY.

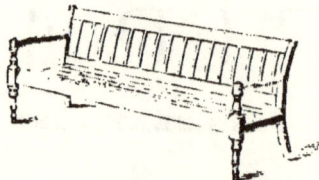

SCHOOL FURNITURE OF ALL VARIETIES OF STYLE AND FINISH.

Teachers' Desks, Chairs, Settees, Blackboards, Etc.

Church Furniture, Settees for Churches, Sabbath Schools, Halls, etc., twenty varieties. Pews complete, or ends separately.

ESTIMATES GIVEN FOR WORK, DELIVERED AT ANY POINT.

Satisfaction guaranteed and all Work warranted.

M. W. CHASE, 212 and 214 Seventh St., BUFFALO, N. Y.

SEND FOR CATALOGUE AND PRICE LIST.

BARNES, BANCROFT & CO.

RETAILERS, IMPORTERS AND JOBBERS OF

DRY GOODS AND CARPETS

The Great Cash Retail House of Western New York.

Nos. 260, 262, 264, 266 and 268 MAIN STREET,

BUFFALO, N. Y.

THE COURIER COMPANY,

Proprietors and Publishers of the

DAILY COURIER

Six issues per week, $10.00 per annum.

Seven issues per week, $12.00 per annum.

Sunday issue $2.50 per annum.

THE WEEKLY COURIER,

Published every Wednesday, $1.00 per annum.

THE EVENING REPUBLIC

$5.00 per annum, or single copies two cents.

SUBSCRIPTIONS INVARIABLY IN ADVANCE.

TERMS OF ADVERTISING MADE KNOWN AT THE COUNTING ROOM.

The Commercial and Marine news and the reports of the Live Stock Trade of Buffalo are reported fully in all editions of the Courier and in the Evening Republic.

☞ The statistics in the preceding pages were compiled for and published in the Buffalo Daily and Weekly Courier.

GEO. I. THURSTONE & CO.

→❀ DRUGGISTS, ❀←

416 MAIN STREET (American Block), BUFFALO, N. Y.

MANUFACTURERS AND DEALERS IN RELIABLE

DRUGS, MEDICINES AND TOILET ARTICLES

OUR PRESCRIPTION DEPARTMENT receives special attention. It is supplied with the best quality of remedies that can be obtained, and so regulated as to preclude the possibility of a mistake.

"PURE WINES AND LIQUORS FOR MEDICINAL USE."

We would call particular attention to our PERFUMERY and FANCY GOODS, our stock being the largest and most complete in this city, consisting of FRENCH, ENGLISH and AMERICAN HANDKERCHIEF EXTRACTS, COLOGNES, SOAPS, SACHET POWDERS and TOILET ARTICLES.

HAIR, TOOTH, NAIL and other BRUSHES in great variety.

SPONGES, CHAMOIS, PUFF BOXES, MIRRORS, CUT GLASS COLOGNE BOTTLES, PUNGENTS, ATOMIZERS, &c., &c.

TELEPHONE.

J. L. CHICHESTER,

BLANK BOOK MANUFACTURER

263 and 265 Washington Street, BUFFALO. N. Y.

RULING, PRINTING AND BINDING.

MARTIN TAYLOR.   CHARLES HERGER.

MARTIN TAYLOR & CO.

PUBLISHERS, BOOKSELLERS AND STATIONERS

22 and 24 WEST EAGLE STREET,

Cor. W. Eagle, Pearl and Niagara Streets.   BUFFALO, N. Y.

CHARLES H. KALBFLEISCH.   ALBERT M. KALBFLEISCH.   FRANKLIN H. KALBFLEISCH.

ESTABLISHED 1829.

MARTIN KALBFLEISCH'S SONS,

MANUFACTURING CHEMISTS

55 Fulton St., New York.   90 Main St., Buffalo, N. Y.

WORKS AT BROOKLYN, N. Y., BUFFALO, N. Y., BAYONNE, N. J.

JAY PETTIBONE & CO.

DISTILLERS

REFINERS, MANUFACTURERS AND WHOLESALE DEALERS IN

BOURBON, MONONGAHELA, RYE AND RECTIFIED WHISKEYS.

Nos. 46, 48 and 50 Lloyd Street, BUFFALO, N. Y.

SHIRRELL & CO.

MANUFACTURERS OF

SHIRRELL'S KULLIYUN WASHING CRYSTAL

THE GREAT LABOR SAVER.

23 MAIN STREET,   BUFFALO, N. Y.

ESTABLISHED 1864

C.GILBERT'S STARCHES

TRADE MARK

ARE ABSOLUTELY PURE.

OFFICE AND SALESROOMS, Nos. 41 and 43 EXCHANGE ST., BUFFALO, N. Y.

WORLD'S PRIZE MEDALS

LONDON, 1862.   PARIS, 1867.   VIENNA, 1873.

Gold Medal United States; Decoration Grand Gold Cross of Honor, Vienna, 1873; Gold Medal of Progress, 1873; Santiago, 1875; Philadelphia, 1876; Paris, 1878; Santiago, 1879; Maryland Institute, 1878; International Industrial Exhibition, Chicago, 1878; American Institute, 1878, awarded

F. S. PEASE,

FOR MAKING THE BEST

LUBRICATING AND ILLUMINATING OILS

IN THE WORLD.

"PEASE'S PREMIUM OIL"

U. S. Government Photometric Tests show that Pease's Premium Oil gives a light equal to 32 sperm candles, making this the most powerful and brilliant hydro-carbon illuminator in the world.

HIGH FIRE TEST !   COLORLESS !   and ODORLESS !

For burning in ORDINARY KEROSENE LAMPS. Endorsed by the highest authority in the United States and Europe.

GERMAN STUDENT LAMP

Consumers can procure the most powerful and brilliant light in existence by its use.

ORDER DIRECT FROM

F. S. PEASE, Manufacturer of OIL

65 and 67 Main Street, 82, 84 and 86 Washington Street,

BUFFALO, N. Y.

PROPRIETOR AND ONLY MANUFACTURER OF THE CELEBRATED BRAND

"PEASE'S PREMIUM OIL."

TO OUT-OF-TOWN CONSUMERS—Send your orders direct to us.

www.ingramcontent.com/pod-product-compliance
Lightning Source LLC
Chambersburg PA
CBHW031817090426
42739CB00008B/1307